THE LITTLE BOOKROOM
GUIDE TO

Paris
with
Children

D0037257

THE LITTLE BOOKROOM
GUIDE TO

Paris with Children

PLAY • EAT • SHOP • STAY

KIM HORTON LEVESQUE

THE LITTLE BOOKROOM
NEW YORK

© 2013 Kim Horton Levesque
Photos © Kim Horton Levesque (unless noted adjacent to photo)
Design: Katy Homans
Cover illustration: Julie Marabelle, www.juliemarabelle.com

A sincere thank you to Matt, to my parents, Roy and Donna Horton, and to my
gracious and most patient editor, Angela Hederman, for all of your support.

Library of Congress Cataloging-in-Publication Data
Levesque, Kim Horton.
The Little Bookroom guide to Paris with children / by Kim Horton Levesque.
p. cm.
Includes bibliographical references and index.
ISBN 1-892145-98-7 (alk. paper)
1. Paris (France)—Guidebooks. 2. Family recreation—France—Paris—Guidebooks.
3. Children—Travel—France—Paris—Guidebooks. I. Title. II. Title: Guide to
Paris with children.
DC708.L3987 2012
914.4'361048412—dc23
                              2012006716

Printed in the United States of America

Published by The Little Bookroom
435 Hudson Street, Suite 300
New York NY 10014
editorial@littlebookroom.com
www.littlebookroom.com

ISBN 978-1-892145-98-7

2468097531

FOR

Juliette, Charlotte, and Madeleine

Contents

As parents, we often idealize what a trip abroad with our children might be. My own planning is usually sprinkled with visions of joyful family bonding with Europe's most magnificent scenery serving as the backdrop; in this case, Paris. My daydreams however, transcend a visit to the Eiffel Tower, the Mona Lisa, or the Arc de Triomphe. I have a grand notion that my child's exposure to great art, incredible food, sublime scenery, and the sound of a new language will ignite their curiosity and inspire a lifetime of learning. If you've picked up this guide, you may have entertained similar ideas. Traveling with three young children, I've found that our most enjoyable trips are nurtured by this idealism; once we've arrived, however, they are powered by pragmatism.

Taking your kids abroad is an exercise in letting go — of schedules, of expectations, of control. Jet lag, fatigue, low blood sugar, even the tap water, conspire together to bring out the worst in even the best and most patient of us, but traveling to Paris with children is easier than you think if you have realistic expectations. Familiarize yourself with the elation, as well as the inherent frustrations, of traveling with kids — and make peace with them.

Once you've committed to taking your children overseas, make them a part of the trip planning process regardless of their age. Parents can inspire interest beforehand by visiting monuments virtually or by viewing museum collections online. In *Paris with Children*, I've provided helpful hints and specific directions to assist in navigating French as well as English-language websites. **You may notice that some of the websites listed in this guide do not have the prefix www as part of their web addresses.** This is not a mistake; in fact, the links will not work if the prefix is added.

I've organized this guide around Paris's most identifiable monuments instead of the capital's 20 districts or arrondissements. Louvre-Tuileries-Opéra can be more useful than the designations 1st, 2nd, and 9th, especially for a parent who, unfamiliar with Paris, steps out of a cab, bus, or Métro station with a hungry or exhausted child—I want to be sure families can find cafés and restaurants quickly. I've selected bakeries, cafés, and casual restaurants with food that appeals to children. I've tried to avoid chains, especially non-French ones, but as most parents know, in a moment of desperation, we will resort to just about anything. Don't be surprised if your kids crave what they eat at home; the mere touchdown on French soil doesn't inspire a gastronomical epiphany, especially in wee ones. France's baby boom of recent years means more children are seen in cafés, bistros, and restaurants. And while the stiff, inflexible decorum of yesteryear appears to be loosening, keep in mind that French culture is still a relatively formal one in which children are expected to be well-behaved at the table.

Practically speaking, one major monument or museum a day plus one child-centered activity is an enjoyable pace at which to see the city. It can be adjusted of course, depending on the age of your children and your own ambition. Within the entry for each monument, museum, and landmark I've included brief details and facts, a bit about the history and highlights, so that parents can provide their children with an interesting introduction to what they're seeing. I've also listed parks and playgrounds near major attractions to help make sightseeing easier for families.

Jet lag can be disheartening for everyone, especially for families traveling with children younger than 3 years old. It can last anywhere from two to seven days depending on your home time zone. Kids may feel disoriented as their biological clocks readjust. Sunlight and rest can help alleviate some of the symptoms, but don't be surprised if, after pulling one or more all-nighters with the kids, your days begin in the afternoon. Traveling from the western U.S., my daughters have always awakened at midnight local time, ready to play for an eight-hour stretch. Sleep would eventually follow from 9am to 3pm. With this in mind, I've noted which restaurants serve meals continuously so that your family can eat outside of France's rigid meal times (usually 11:30am–2pm for lunch and 7–10pm for dinner; most brasseries offer food service all day). Remember it's still rare to find a high chair in the city; what you'll see more often in cafés and casual restaurants are parents feeding children who are seated in their strollers.

The first jet-lagged days are an ideal time to visit museums (the Louvre, Musée d'Orsay, and Musée du Quai Branly among many others) that keep evening hours at least once a week—kids are wide awake and tourist traffic is lighter at these times. The Paris Museum Pass can be a useful tool for families with museum-heavy itineraries. While most museums and monuments are free for those under 18 years of age, the pass allows adults entry, without queuing, to more than 60 sights during a specified period of time. The Paris Museum Pass website has an easy-to-use, interactive map of museums and sights that provides opening hours for included sights: www.paris-museumpass.com (see page 65 for a more detailed discussion of the pass).

Don't forget about Wednesday afternoons when most French children finish school early. More workshops and activities are offered then, but lines are longer. If you're hoping for your children to interact with local children, don't expect to see many older kids in the parks unless it's one of the official school holidays (dates for the annual holidays are listed on the Ministry of Education's national website: www.education.gouv.fr — choose the *le calendrier scolaire* link). School vacations also mean more crowds at tourist sights and at the amusement parks near Paris — Disneyland Paris and Parc Astérix (page 370, 373).

The lack of restrooms in Paris has long been a source of anxiety for parents of young children. For this reason, I've included the location of public facilities closest to major sights. French café and restaurant staff aren't as laissez-faire with their WCs as in some countries — stopping in just to use the WC will, more often than not, be met with an intimidating and disapproving stare — those who use the restrooms are expected to buy something. Even fast-food venues, once friendly to toilet-training parents, have made their restrooms more difficult to access. In most, the cashier will provide customers with a token that unlocks the WC or a restroom code will be disclosed on the receipt. Thankfully, the city's public restrooms have become easier to find. There are now more than 400 freestanding, self-cleaning *sanisettes* around Paris (for a list of locations, see www.paris.fr, type *sanisette* in the search box). Public lavatories, indicated by a blue-and-white sign and the word *toilettes,* charge a nominal fee for use (,20€–,40€, cash only) and have attendants who monitor and maintain the facility.

Plan and prepare for downtime: arts and crafts, coloring, watching French cartoons, or reading — anything that helps your child feel comfortable in their new environment. If you've forgotten to pack safety scissors and glue sticks, head to a Monoprix store. Similar to the Target chain in the U.S., Monoprix has a useful selection of art supplies; it also carries children's clothing, gear, baby care items, and groceries. Downtime is remarkably easier in an apartment rental where there are kitchen amenities and space to move about. This guide provides contact information for rental agencies as well as a list of critical questions to ask before renting. Flats offer a more authentic glimpse into everyday life in the capital by allowing families to interact with Parisians as neighbors. Parents who feel as if they aren't seeing as much of the city as they would like can alternate spending low-key moments at home with the kids while the other visits the city.

Paris isn't just the ultimate shopping destination for adults—it's also a rich trove of brilliant children's fashion boutiques and creative designers. In *Paris with Children*, I've directed readers to the capital's best independent stores, ones that offer a spectrum of prices and styles. I've also included an overview of French chains for kids' clothing. Both have a selection of quintessentially French styles as well as more modern interpretations of children's fashion. Be sure to check the shops' websites—many of them feature inspiring look-book sections filled with chic, fashion-forward ideas for your little ones.

୧ର

One of the best things about traveling with kids is that they force you to do things you wouldn't have done otherwise. In my case I've fancied myself too sophisticated a traveler to do something as embarrassingly touristy as having a portrait made at place du Tertre, in Paris's Montmartre district. Enter my 6-year-old daughter. Within 45 seconds of walking into the square, Madeleine had talked me

into it, and was seated before an artist. Immediately I found myself overcome with an acute sense of joy, understanding that we were indelibly recording the collection of extraordinary moments that we had shared that day in ink . . . in chalk. Madeleine had taken me off-checklist and on an unanticipated detour to what she wanted to see and do: an obscure park, a children's shop, a crêpe stand, and finally a portrait in place du Tertre.

Photos end up piled in drawers, at least mine do. Paintings, especially ones of your child, are framed and hung. I had gone to Paris to share my favorite city with my daughters, to take them down discreet, off-the-beaten-path streets. This day I had planned to show "my" Paris to Madeleine—instead she shared hers with me.

Be open to the Paris your child wants to see.

RENTING AN APARTMENT

Short-term apartment rentals provide the most practical, convenient, and cost-effective option for family accommodations in Paris. Finding a flat for a couple or small family is simple, but choices narrow considerably for families of five or more. The search can be time consuming; the larger the apartment required, the earlier the search needs to begin.

Apartments can be booked through rental agencies or through websites that bypass the third party, connecting potential tenants directly with owners. An accredited agency offers a degree of facility, security, and recourse. Many will arrange reliable and affordable airport transfers, an invaluable service for those with little ones. Agencies will usually send the apartment key with the driver, which helps in sorting through the exhausting logistics of dragging jet-lagged kids first to the agency's office, then to the apartment. Having a driver arranged in advance is also useful when arriving in Paris at an off-hour.

Most agency websites provide comprehensive information on individual apartments. Ask for the exact address before renting and check the location on maps.google.com. The zoom feature is available for most addresses. This tool allows renters to see the street, building, neighborhood, and amenities such as nearby parks and shops.

If the following information is not specified in the listing, be sure to verify it with an agency representative:

- What floor is the apartment on? (Carrying a 30-pound toddler up six flights of stairs several times a day becomes tiresome.)

- Is there an elevator?

- What is the square footage of the apartment?

- Is electricity included in the rental price or is it billed separately?

- What form of deposit is accepted—cash, money order, U.S. personal check, or a credit-card hold? Credit cards can be ideal because of the fraud protection often included; they also allow tenants to avoiding wiring potentially large amounts of cash to the owner's foreign bank account.

- Are clients required to take out apartment insurance to cover potential damage? If so, check with your insurance company to see if this type of coverage is included in an umbrella or homeowner's policy.

- Do the bedroom windows face a noisy street? Is the apartment above a noisy bar or restaurant?

- Is the apartment located directly over a Métro line (the rumble and vibrations can upset sensitive sleepers)?

- Is there a discount offered on longer stays?

- Is there any feature that is unsafe in the apartment for young children; i.e., loft, balcony, or windows without childproof locks?

- Is it a nonsmoking apartment?

- Are pets allowed (for those with allergies or pets)?

- How far is the nearest supermarket?

- What is the closest Métro stop?
- Is there a washer and dryer? (Many apartments are only equipped with a washing machine.)
- If important, is satellite television with English channels available?
- Is there a separate charge for Internet service?
- Is the apartment air-conditioned?
- Are all linens provided?
- Can housekeeping arrangements be made, or are they included in the rental charge?

The Paris Convention and Visitors Bureau's English website, en.parisinfo.com, provides a list of Aparthotels, apartment-style rooms with hotel amenities, as well as more than 20 agencies that rent furnished apartments. The 1st, 4th, 5th, 6th, and 7th arrondissements are within walking distance of Paris's top sights, making them the most convenient for families.

Below are agencies that, in past dealings, have been reliable.

Ah Paris, www.ahparis.com

Book a Flat, www.book-a-flat.com

Chez Vous, www.chezvous.com

Haven in Paris, www.haveninparis.com

Locaflat, www.locaflat.com

My Apartment in Paris, www.my-apartment-in-paris.com

New York Habitat, www.nyhabitat.com

Paris Attitude, www.parisattitude.com

Paris Hideaways, studio.provaction.com

Paris Perfect, www.parisperfect.com

Websites like Vacation Rental By Owner, www.vrbo.com and France USA Contacts, www.fusac.fr, offer classified-style listings. Potential renters can contact owners directly regarding their properties.

CHILDREN & FRENCH FOOD

Some parents entertain the fantasy that France is a land of gastro-nomic epiphany, that touching down on French soil will begin a sudden and life-altering evolution of their children's palate. Not so. In France, good taste of the culinary variety is nurtured from infancy at home, institutionalized in school meals, and consistently reinforced both socially and culturally—not developed overnight. It begins when babies have their initial tastes of homemade purées or commercial baby foods. Many first French foods are those also familiar to American or British babies—peas, carrots, potatoes—but others may raise many an anglophone's brow: artichokes, ratatouille, and vegetables de Provence.

At six months they progress to more complex mélanges: cod and carrots, veal and squash, salmon with rice and vegetables, veal with green beans in cream sauce, or lamb with mixed veggies. As kids grow, blends made with Gruyère and Emmental cheese, duck, trout, turkey, and sole are introduced (www.bledina.com, www.babybio.fr, www.bebe.nestle.fr).

By the time they reach elementary school, most French children have been exposed to a wide variety of foods through public lunch menus. Menus are an important part of the weekly ritual; administrators post them each Monday outside of schools and online. The typical midday meal includes four to five courses: Monday: fresh grapefruit, vegetable omelette, green beans, organic yogurt, chocolate cream puff; Tuesday: salad with white and red cabbage, braised beef, green peas, Cantal cheese, pineapple; Wednesday: lentil salad, roast turkey, organic cauliflower, Morbier cheese, banana; Thursday: red cabbage in vinaigrette, sole in tomato sauce, organic rice, goat cheese, fruit salad; Friday: tabouli, sautéed turkey in mustard sauce, carrots, Edam cheese, organic clementines (taken from a French school lunch menu, Caisse des Écoles, 17th arrondissement, www.mairie17.paris.fr; see *Le 17e au quotidien* then *Enseignement-Cantine* tabs). District dietitians also prepare recommended dinner menus for parents, complete with recipes, each week. The idea is to pro-

mote a balanced and seasonally mindful diet outside of school, where kids will eat more than 75% of their meals.

Parents hoping that the Atlantic will provide the buffer necessary to break their child's addiction to comfort foods may be out of luck. Unfortunately *nuggets de poulet* and *hamburgers* are now common items on children's menus in France. It's still rare, however, to find macaroni and cheese or grilled (cheddar) cheese outside of a specialty cheese shop or the Grande Épicerie at the Bon Marché (page 255).

But while the palate of petit Parisians may be more evolved than their anglophone counterparts, it's still uncommon to see young children in the city's finer restaurants. Formal meals typically last two-and-a-half to three hours, too long for wee ones in any country to hold still and mind their manners. Families with children of all ages, however, are well represented at cafés and bistros.

As parents, we choose our battles cautiously. Presenting new foods to a picky eater, understandably, may not be a struggle for which we have the time or energy. Rest assured there are plenty of delicious options for fresh pizza, hamburgers made from French Charolais beef, and spaghetti in Paris. Most restaurants will also prepare pasta with butter or *steak haché* (ground beef patty) upon request.

Stay heartened for there will be new foods for which your children will develop a fondness during their time in Paris. The *tartine,* a fresh, toasted baguette slathered in rich butter and seasonal home-made jam, seems to be universally appealing. Observe the *goûter* while in France—a sweet snack eaten by children of all ages (and many parents) around 4pm to help tide them over until dinner. It usually consists of a fresh pastry, cookie, or sweet treat served with fruit juice or water sweetened with flavored syrup. Kids love it. Trying something new, albeit sweet, may begin a trend that opens them up to tasting something savory. It's a baby step down a path that will expand their palate and ultimately broaden their worldview.

A READING LIST FOR CHILDREN & PARENTS

Paris Hide-and-Seek by Masumi (Parigramme, 2009) is my favorite introduction to Paris for children. Other books that our family has found entertaining and enlightening include:

Astérix the Gaul by René Goscinny and Albert Uderzo, illustrator (Orion, 2004) and all the other Astérix books.

Eloise in Paris by Kay Thompson and Hilary Knight, illustrator (Simon & Schuster, 1999).

Everybody Bonjours by Leslie Kimmelman and Sarah McMenemy, illustrator (Knopf Books for Young Readers, 2008).

A Kid's Guide to the Louvre for Adults by Isabelle Bonithon Courant (Le Baron Perché, 2009).

Madeline by Ludwig Bemelmans (Viking Juvenile, 2000).

Marie from Paris by Françoise Sabatier-Morel and Isabelle Pellegrini (ABC Melody Éditions, 2011). Available from www.fnac.com

Mini Masters Boxed Set: *Dancing with Degas*, *A Picnic with Monet*, *A Magical Day with Matisse* and *In the Garden with Van Gogh* by Julie Merberg and Suzanne Bober (Chronicle Books, 2006).

Mon Cahier de Coloriage Paris, *The Paris Coloring Book*, by Isabelle Chemin (Parigramme, 2010).

Mon Livre Animé: Paris by Géraldine Krasinski and Emmanuel Ristord (Éditions Milan, 2011).This interactive, pull-the-tab, pop-out book takes children to Paris's most famous sights and monuments. Available from www.fnac.com

Monuments that Tell Stories of Paris by Jean Daly (Parigramme, 2009).

Mr. Chicken Goes to Paris by Leigh Hobbs (Bloomsbury Publishing, 2010).

Objective Louvre: The Guide to Family Visits by Frédéric Morvan (Musée du Louvre Éditions, 2008).

Rendez-vous with France: A Point and Pronounce Guide to Traveling, Shopping and Eating by Jill Butler (Globe Pequot, 2002).

A PLAYLIST FOR CHILDREN & PARENTS

Some of the best classic songs for children:

"For me Formidable," Charles Aznavour

"Les Champs Élysées," Joe Dassin

"Comic Strip," Serge Gainsbourg

"La Vie en Rose," Edith Piaf

"Au clair de la lune" (various artists; choose your favorite version)

"Fais dodo" (various artists; choose your favorite version)

"Sur le pont d'Avignon" (various artists; choose your favorite version)

Putumayo Presents: French Playground (Putumayo World Music, 2005)

For teens interested in contemporary French music:

Ben l'Oncle Soul

Brigitte

Zaz

MC Solaar

Les Nubians

Coeur de Pirate (Quebecois, but extremely popular in France)

IAM

Louise Attaque

THE MÉTRO & TAXIS

Kids love the Métro. With infants and toddlers, it's most easily navigated using a baby carrier, but you will see plenty of Parisian parents hauling their strollers and buggies, with children seated inside, up and down the stairs each day. Some Métro stations have doors next to the turnstiles to facilitate entrance; signaling the agent in the booth to unlock the doors, however, can be a feat at times. If the train or bus is full, parents are expected to fold their stroller. Children under 4 years old ride for free on Paris's public transportation system and those younger than 10 years old receive a 50% reduction on tickets and 10-pack ticket *carnets*.

Taxis can be a lifesaver when an unexpected rainstorm dampens travel plans or when kids or parents are too tired for a long walk or subway ride home. In Paris, it's extremely difficult to hail a cab in the middle of the street as they are often full. Find the nearest official taxi stand indicated by the word Taxi inside a blue rectangle. A map with all of the taxi stands in Paris can be downloaded from the city's French website, www.paris.fr. Type in *taxi station* and follow the links to the pdf file. Alternatively, buy the detailed *Paris Pratique Par Arrondissement* street map book, also known as *l'Indispensable*, at a magazine stand or department store; be sure to choose the one that indicates that it includes taxi stands (from 5€).

Taxis can also be reserved in advance by calling one of the following taxi services that have an English-speaking operator available. Remember when reserving that taxi drivers start the meter as they leave to meet you. Most taxis accommodate a maximum of four passengers; let the operator know the number in your group so they can send a larger *monospace* (minivan) or two cabs if needed.

Paris's central number for taxi dispatch is 01.45.30.30.30.

Alpha Taxis: 01.45.85.85.85, www.alphataxis.fr

Taxis 75: 06.77.26.44.55, www.taxis75.fr

Taxi G7: 01.41.27.66.99, www.taxisg7.com

Traveling from the airports to central Paris is simplest via a private or shared shuttle or taxi, all of which provide door-to-door service. Parents can request infant car seats and boosters when making a reservation; you will usually be asked your child's age, weight, and height so that the appropriate-size seat can be provided. Taxicabs are exempt from car seat regulations so it is rare that they will be equipped with one. Hotels and apartment rental agencies are also good resources for finding reliable transfer services.

Three reliable taxi companies that provide airport-to-city service are:

Allonavette: 01.75.68.01.96, www.allonavette.com

FirstWay, 01.48.63.74.37, www.firstway.fr

Paris Shuttle, 01.53.39.18.18, www.parishuttle.com

PARIS BY BOAT, BUS, BICYCLE, & CAR

Boat Tours

Many companies offer guided boat tours of the Seine and Paris's canals. For a comprehensive week-by-week listing of what's going on in the capital, including a complete list of boat tour companies, see the *Pariscope* or *l'Officiel des Spectacles* entertainment magazines, both available at newspaper stands.

Kids of all ages usually enjoy the one-hour boat cruises that offer an expedient overview of Paris's most famous sights from the comfort of a seat.

Bateaux Mouches, page 328

Bateaux Parisiens, page 302

Batobus (Hop-on, Hop-off Boat Tour), page 185

Canauxrama, page 122

Vedettes du Pont Neuf, page 194

Bus Tours

Balabus, page 117

Paris L'Opentour (Hop-on, Hop-off Bus Tour), page 75

Les Cars Rouges (Hop-on, Hop-off Bus Tour), page 302

Bicycle Tours

Bike About Tours, page 186

Fat Tire Bike Tours, page 303

Car Tour

4 Roues Sous 1 Parapluie, page 51

Tours Outside of Paris

Three well-established tour companies offer day and overnight trips to destinations outside of Paris including Giverny, Mont St-Michel, Loire Valley castles, and the Normandy D-Day beaches: Cityrama, www.cityrama.com; Paris Vision, www.parisvision.com; France Tourisme, www.francetourisme.fr. The experience can be hit or miss depending on the tour guide, but it's a practical way to avoid the hassle of renting and driving a car.

RAINY DAY IDEAS

When rainy weather demands a change in the day's plans, museums are a convenient option. Here are several more suggestions:

Tour Montparnasse (see page 241)

Cité des Enfants (see page 347)

Le Grand Rex (see page 52)

Cirque d'Hiver Bouglione (see page 126)

École Ritz Escoffier (see page 51)

WH Smith (see page 108)

Yoga Enfants–Melanie Yoga Fitness (see page 242)

The American Library in Paris (see page 301)

Musée Grévin (see page 72)

Les Catacombes de Paris (see page 235)

Musée des Arts Forains (see page 136)

SEASONAL EVENTS FOR FAMILIES

Spring

Carnaval de Paris is a relatively tame yet colorful parade that brightens the city streets during traditional Carnival time, at the end of February through the beginning of March. Its origins are linked to Paris's medieval Fête des Fous celebration (www.carnavaldeparis.org).

Foire du Trône is a two-month long, county-style fun fair that takes place from April to June at the Pelouse de Reuilly in the western end of Bois de Vincennes (www.foiredutrone.com).

La Nuit des Musées is an evening in mid-May when more than 2,000 museums throughout Europe keep exceptionally late hours, some until 1am. Virtually all of Paris's museums participate in the celebration with special concerts, shows, and exhibits. Events can be found on the website by selecting city and typing Paris in the search box (www.nuitdesmusees.culture.fr).

Salon de l'agriculture brings provincial France to Paris's Porte de Versailles exhibition hall (15th arrondissement). Nearly 5,000 farm animals are available for children to see: cows, bulls, horses, goats, pigs, dogs, and sheep. There are hundreds of opportunities to taste and discover the best in culinary products from each region (www.salon-agriculture.com).

Summer

Bastille Day festivities are observed each July 14th. It is a day of national pride celebrated in grand style with a military parade on the Champs-Élysées and with fireworks near the Eiffel Tower, best viewed from Trocadéro and the Champ-de-Mars. Street revelry keeps Paris abuzz on July 14th, while bars, clubs, restaurants, and Seine boat cruises offer festive menus for customers (www.paris.fr).

La Fête Foraine du Jardin des Tuileries is a popular summertime carnival that lasts from June to August in the Tuileries gardens. It features more than 60 county-fair style rides, food stands, and game booths (www.feteforaine-jardindestuileries.com).

Les Grandes Eaux Musicales are planned on weekends and on several holidays from April through the end of October, from 9am to 6:30pm. Music plays and fountains flow as visitors walk Versailles's spectacular grounds. Check the website for specific water program times as well as musical fountain programs on certain summer Tuesdays. (www.chateauversaillesspectacles.fr, Adults 18€; 6–17 years 6,5€; 5 and under free).

During **Les Grandes Eaux Nocturnes**, visitors stroll the gardens at the Versailles palace on summer evenings against a backdrop of music, colorful lights, and flowing fountains. The events take place Saturdays between 9pm and 11:20pm from late June to the beginning of September. A fireworks show begins around 11pm (www.chateauversaillesspectacles.fr, adults 23€; 6–17 years 19€; 5 and under free).

Paris Plages transforms a portion of the Seine's Right Bank into a sandy beach for those who can't get away from the city, in late July. Outdoor concerts and water attractions are a mainstay of this month-long festival during what is typically Paris's hottest month. Swimming in the river isn't allowed, but there are plenty of opportunities for water sport and play near Bassin de la Villette in the 19th arrondissement (www.paris.fr).

Jean-François Deroubaix/Gamma-Rapho via Getty Images

Les Pestacles is a series of child-themed, Wednesday-afternoon concerts and activities organized in the Parc Floral inside the Bois de Vincennes. The festival opens in June and lasts through mid-September (www.lespestacles.fr).

Fall

La Fête au Bois de Boulogne is a giant fair that takes place in late August through early October, with hundreds of rides, food stands, and game stalls. The closest Métro stop is Rue de la Pompe (www.lafeteaubois.com).

La Fête de la Science is a national celebration of science in mid- to late-October. The public of all ages is invited to participate in workshops, experiments, and activities at venues throughout the city in an effort to stimulate interest in all branches of science. A French-only schedule is available online (www.fetedelascience.fr).

Les Fêtes du Miel honey festival is held each year at the end of September at the Luxembourg Garden Apiary. Honey is sold and the apiary is open for touring and discovery. In early October, Parc Georges-Brassens (15th arrondissement) hosts the honey festival (www.la-sca.net).

Les Journées du Patrimoine is a two-day event that celebrates France's cultural heritage. National monuments that are usually closed to the public open their doors during the third weekend of September (www.journeesdupatrimoine.culture.fr).

Mon Premier Festival is a film festival organized for youth that takes place during La Toussaint school vacation (All Saints' Day) at the end of October through early November. It's designed to inspire interest in film for children 2 years and older. A handful of British and American movies are always shown in VO (Version Originale) during the festival (www.monpremierfestival.org).

Salon du Chocolat assembles scores of French chocolatiers at this enormous chocolate expo that is open to the public. It takes place each October at the Porte de Versailles Exhibition Center and features chocolate tastings, demonstrations, and exhibits. Chocoland, a special area set up for children 4–10 years old, offers hands-on workshops every 30 minutes throughout the day (www.salonduchocolat.fr).

Winter

Chinese New Year is the occasion for a huge annual parade along with other festivities organized in the 13th arrondissement; it's best with children 10 years and older (www.paris.fr).

Festival Ciné Junior is an annual festival during which French and international films of particular interest to children and youth are featured; it lasts for two weeks in February. Movies are categorized by age and shown in their original language with subtitles (VO); there are selections programmed for 3- to 6-year-olds, 7- to 10-year-olds, and children 11 years and older (www.cinemapublic.org).

Salon Playtime is an international trade show dedicated to fashion, gear, art, and other products for infants, children, and expecting parents. Attendance is limited to trade professionals, but the salon's website provides links to exhibitors which include some of the most creative and cutting-edge designers and manufacturers in the industry. The show arrives sometime in late January to early February (www.playtimeparis.com).

Winter Holidays

Winter holidays in Paris are magical. Each year Parisians celebrate the season with holiday markets, decorative lights, over-the-top department store window displays, ice skating rinks, and festive carousels. The office of tourism's website keeps an up-to-date list of current events (en.parisinfo.com).

Notable Christmas light displays: avenue des Champs-Élysées (8th arr.), avenue Montaigne (8th arr.), Place Vendôme (1st arr.), Les Halles (1st arr.), Viaduc des Arts (12th arr.), Bercy Village (12th arr.).

Notable department store window displays: Galeries Lafayette (9th arr.), Printemps (9th arr.), Le Bon Marché (7th arr.), and BHV (4th arr.).

Christmas markets (Marchés de Noël): Trocadéro (16th arr.), Champs-Élysées (8th arr.), Saint Germain des Prés (6th arr.), Montparnasse (15th arr.), La Défense, the Latin Quarter (5th arr.), and many others.

Merry-go-rounds: Free holiday carousels are set up in each arrondissement for the public to enjoy in mid-December and include Hôtel de Ville plaza (4th arr.), Square du Temple (3rd arr.), Place de l'Odéon (6th arr.), Square Bonsergent (10th arr.), Place du Trocadéro (16th arr.), Square Louise-Michel (18th arr., Montmartre) among others. The lighted carousels are open from 10am to 7pm.

Ice-skating rinks: Hôtel de Ville plaza (4th arr.), first floor of the Eiffel Tower (7th arr.), Stade Charlety (13th arr.).

New Year's Eve (*réveillon de la Saint-Sylvestre* or *réveillon du jour de l'an*) is celebrated throughout the capital with champagne, foie gras, festive dinners, cocktails, and dancing. With children, the celebration is best enjoyed from an apartment or hotel room with a view of the Eiffel Tower; the fireworks show that illuminates the tower at midnight is thrilling.

BILINGUAL SUMMER DAY CAMPS

Vacation day camp programs exist in many of Paris's most well-regarded bilingual schools—and these day camps are open to children visiting from abroad. Academic, sports, and art-themed programs that use English as the language of instruction offer week-to-week enrollment during school holidays.

The following is a list of schools that offer bilingual summer vacation camps for English speakers in preschool through high school. Students who are currently enrolled in these schools have registration priority so be sure to contact the schools well in advance for admission information.

International School of Paris
6, rue Beethoven, 16th arr.
01.42.24.09.54
M Passy
www.isparis.edu
The Holiday Language Program is available to students from ages 3 to 18. The ISP Holiday Language Program offers courses in French and English on a weekly basis from July 4 to July 29.

American School of Paris

41, rue Pasteur, Saint Cloud, 92210
01.41.12.82.82
www.asparis.org

Students from around the world share in a well-rounded, interdisciplinary program during their summer holiday. Classes in English are offered for students from ages 4 to 18. The school is located in a Parisian suburb, approximately 10 miles from city center (transportation options on website).

The Bilingual Montessori School of Paris

65, Quai d'Orsay, 7th arr.
01.45.55.13.27
RER: Pont de l'Alma
www.montessori-paris.com

This Montessori school's summer program is offered on a week-to-week basis for children 3-6 years old. The curriculum includes art, music, cooking, gym, and field trips in Paris. Alternate location: 23, avenue George V, 8th arr., 01.45.55.13.27, **M** Alma-Marceau.

École Montessori Rive Gauche

24, rue de Babylone, 7th arr.
01.45.48.43.97
M Sèvres-Babylone
www.ecolemontessori-rivegauche.com

The helpful staff of this small Left Bank Montessori school welcomes children 2–6 years old into its weekly, bilingual vacation program.

Marymount International School

72, boulevard de la Saussaye, Neuilly Sur Seine, 92200

01.46.24.10.51

M Pont de Neuilly, Pont de Levallois-Becon

www.marymount.fr

Marymount's suburban campus, located 15 minutes from central Paris, offers sports- and art-themed English-language camps for children 4–16 years old in summer.

École Active Bilingue

6, avenue Van Dyck, 8th arr.

01.46.22.14.24

M Courcelles, Monceau

www.eab.fr

EAB's summer workshops for students 4–12 years old feature a range of activities that include intensive language courses in English or French, field trips, sports, art, and cultural activities. Camp location may vary between EAB's other campuses in the 8th, 15th, 16th, and 17th arrondissements.

BABYSITTING SERVICES

A number of options exist for parents who need extra help with their children while in Paris. Most of the palace hotels can arrange babysitting services for their guests. Try connecting with an online English-speaking parent group for personal references — the English Speaking Mums of Paris and Goodnight Moon: An English Language Playgroup in Paris are two groups organized through Meetup.com. Parents in these groups arrange frequent cultural outings and play dates and are an excellent local source for help and information. Begin interviewing potential sitters in advance via e-mail, phone, or Skype if you know that you'll need help during your stay.

American Church in Paris (65, quai d'Orsay, 7th arr., 01.40.62.05.00, www.acparis.org) is an interdenominational gathering ground for expats. They maintain an on-site message board with ads from English-speaking nannies and sitters.

Angloinfo (www.paris.angloinfo.com) has a lengthy list of English-speaking baby sitting service providers under its Family Life & Living in Paris section.

Babychou (6, rue du Docteur Finlay, 15th arr., 01.43.13.33.23, www.babychou.com) is a well-established agency offering babysitting services in hotels.

Babylangues (19, rue Pavée, 4th arr., 08.11.62.08.12, www.babylangues.com) can arrange experienced, English-speaking occasional or part-time childcare.

Déclic Éveil (06.61.06.99.03, www.decliceveil.fr) has received rave reviews as a babysitting service that emphasizes educational and creative activities for children. Sitters can be arranged in advance or on short notice.

France USA Contacts (frwww.fusac.) has a childcare section where offers and requests for employment can be posted.

Yoopies (www.yoopies.fr) is a French website similar to Sittercity.com and Care.com in the U.S., where parents can review babysitters' profiles and read other parents' reviews.

IF YOUR CHILD IS SICK

Emergency Numbers

Police: dial 17

Fire service: dial 18

Ambulance (SAMU): dial 15

SOS Anti-Poison: 01.40.05.48.48 or 01.40.05.45.45

Late-night and English-speaking Pharmacies

Pharmacies supply prescription and non-prescription medicines to the public in France. The symbol of the *pharmacie*, a green cross, makes them easy to spot. Pharmacists are qualified to give medical advice and many of them speak basic English. Many medicines that are available over-the-counter in the U.S are kept behind the counter in France; customers are expected to describe their symptoms to the pharmacist who will then select an appropriate treatment. *Pharmacies* also sell baby care items such as specialized infant formulas, soaps, and lotions. *Parapharmacies* carry many of the same items as *pharmacies* with the exception of prescription medicines. They offer a wider variety of products than *pharmacies* including less expensive options for hygiene and baby care.

French pharmacists will have an easier time identifying any medications you or your children may use if you make sure to note their generic names. Know your child's weight in metric units to be able to follow dosing recommendations (2.2 lbs. = 1 kg.).

Pharmacies where English is spoken

Anglo-American Pharmacy, 37, avenue Marceau, 16th arr., 01.47.20.57.37, **M** Alma-Marceau

British Pharmacy, 62, avenue des Champs-Élysées, 8th arr., 01.43.59.22.52, **M** George V

British Pharmacy Villa Mayor, 1, rue Auber, 9th arr., 01.42.65.88.29, **M** Opéra.

Pharmacy Swann (Anglo-American), 6, rue de Castiglione, 1st arr., 01.42.60.72.96, **M** Tuileries

Useful Vocabulary at the Pharmacie

My child has . . .	Mon enfant a . . .
an earache	mal à l'oreille
a stomach ache	mal au ventre
a headache	mal à la tête
toothache	mal aux dents
sore throat	mal à la gorge
eye pain	mal aux yeux
a fever	de la fièvre
strep throat	la pharyngite
diarrhea	la diarrhée
a cough	une toux
a cold	un rhume
the flu	la grippe
an allergy	une allergie

skin rash	une irritation cutanée
diaper rash	l'érythème fessier
diabetes	le diabète
a burn	une brûlure
my child	mon enfant...
is vomiting	vomit
is constipated	est constipé

Over-the-counter Medicines

Acetaminophen	Paracétamol
Ibuprofen	Ibuprofène
Aspirin	Aspirine
Saline solution to clear congested noses	Sérum Physiologique
Expectorant for older children, other brands are available	Rhinathiol
Diaper cream, other brands are available	Mitosyl
Pedialyte-type electrolyte replacement	Alhydrate, Adiaril
Antihistamine like Benadryl	Antihistaminique
Over-the-counter, without prescription	Sans ordonnance
Prescription	Ordonnance

English-Speaking Hospitals

The United States Embassy in Paris provides a number of useful dossiers including a list of English-speaking doctors and specialists in Paris and throughout France. It can be downloaded at france.usembassy.gov/living_in_france.html.

American Hospital of Paris, 63, boulevard Victor Hugo, 92202 Neuilly sur Seine, www.american-hospital.org, 01.46.41.25.25
The hospital's emergency department is open 24/7. Emergency teams are bilingual and offer care for medical, surgical and dental emergencies.

Hôpital Franco-Britannique, Hertford British Hospital, 4, rue Kléber, 92300 Levallois, www.ihfb.org, 01.47.59.59.59
24-hour pediatric emergency care

French hospitals specializing in pediatric care:

Hôpital Universitaire Necker-Enfants Malades, 149, rue de Sèvres, 15th arr., **M** Duroc, www.hopital-necker.aphp.fr, 01.44.49.40.00

Hôpital Armand-Trousseau, 26, avenue du Docteur Arnold-Netter, 12th arr., **M** Porte de Vincennes, www.aphp.fr/hopital/armand-trousseau/poles-et-services, 01.44.73.74.75

CHILDREN'S CLOTHING CHAINS

Some of the best times to shop in Paris are during the twice-annual sales most often held from mid-January to mid-February and from the end of June to the end of July. The chain stores below have multiple locations throughout the city. A description of each can be found in the SHOP sections of the book at the page noted.

Bonpoint (see page 253, 292)

Catimini (see page 102)

Du Pareil Au Même (DPAM) (see page 257)

Jacadi (see page 103)

Natalys (see page 264)

Obaïbi-Okaïdi (see page 101)

Petit Bateau (see page 174)

Tartine et Chocolat (see page 296)

Tati (see page 269)

PLAY

EAT

SHOP

STAY

Louvre Tuileries Opéra

PLAY

4 Roues Sous 1 Parapluie

Departs from Place de la Concorde, 8th arr.; hotel pickup in 1st, 2nd, 8th, or 9th arr. also available.

06.67.32.26.68

M Porte de Saint-Ouen

www.4roues-sous-1parapluie.com

See Paris by car with 4 Roues Sous 1 Parapluie, a company that offers tours in a vintage Citroën with an English-speaking driver-tour guide. Each convertible Citroën 2CV can accommodate up to three people and multiple cars may be reserved. The 30-minute Champs-Élysées tour includes a view of Place de la Concorde, the Arc de Triomphe, the Eiffel Tower, Invalides, the Petit and Grand Palais, and the Madeleine church (20€ per person for three; 30€ per person for two; 60€ for one person). The 90-minute Essential Paris tour picks passengers up at their hotel or apartment and takes them past all of the city's major monuments, excluding Montmartre (60€ per person for three; 90€ per person for two; 180€ for one).

École Ritz Escoffier

15, place Vendôme, 1st arr.

01.43.16.30.50

M Tuileries, Opéra

www.ritzparis.com

Wednesday 2:30–5pm

100€

The prestigious Ritz Escoffier cooking school offers a variety of 2½-hour culinary workshops. In La Cuisine des Ritz Kids, children work alongside professional chefs to learn and practice the basics; a translator is provided so the course is perfectly accessible to English speakers. The Ritz Kids program is suitable for ages 6-12, Toque Juniors for ages 12-17. Parents can stay to snap a photo of their chef-in-training as they don the classic uniform complete with a Ritz-embossed toque (plan to arrive 15 minutes early to change), but kids are on their own for the remainder of the class. Fruit juice and pastries are served as snacks and a sample of their work is boxed up to take home. Recent workshops have included: My First Tart (chocolate and caramel tart); vanilla and raspberry macarons; Mon Croc Monsieur (vegetarian croque monsieur); and Galettes Salées (savory crêpes with smoked salmon and goat cheese).

On the website, scheduled classes are described, proposed menus are posted, and reservations may be made.

Le Grand Rex

1, boulevard Poissonière, 2nd arr.
01.45.08.93.89
M Bonne Nouvelle
www.legrandrex.com
Wednesday–Sunday 10am–7pm; daily 10am–7pm (July 1–September 4 and during school holidays)
Adults 9,5€; under 12 years 8€
Audio guide in English is available; best for children ages 7 and older
Go behind the screen, literally, of Le Grand Rex to discover the history of Europe's largest movie theater. Les Étoiles du Rex, an interactive 50-minute audio guided tour, leads visitors past the art deco façade into a stunning theater, with a ceiling lit up by "stars," that seats up to 2,650 people on three levels. Opened in 1932, Le Grand Rex is still

popular as a cinema and concert venue. The special effects and projection room make the tour especially fun for kids as they experience first-hand the magical side of movie making. The guided visit can be combined with a discounted ticket to a current film.

In France, foreign films are shown in either VO, Version Originale (the film's original language with French subtitles) or VF, which means it has been dubbed in French. From time to time, Le Grand Rex will feature a blockbuster in VO. Check the movie section at the expat website Angloinfo: paris.angloinfo.com/information/movies. asp, which lists all films playing in VO throughout Paris.

Jardin des Enfants aux Halles

105, rue Rambuteau, 1st arr.

01.45.08.07.18

M Les Halles, Étienne Marcel

Monday–Friday 9am–sunset; Saturday–Sunday 9am–sunset

(Partially open; project scheduled to be completed in 2013.)

One of the neighborhood's best-loved attractions for children, the Jardin des Enfants (formerly known as Jardin Lalanne) was closed and demolished in 2011 as the city continued its massive renovation plan of Les Halles and the area immediately surrounding it. New plans include two modern playgrounds with innovative structures and spaces, one for 2- to 6-year-olds, the other for 7- to 12-year-olds. A temporary, less elaborate playground has been installed across from the entrance to the church of St-Eustache, next to place René-Cassin. Even in its transitional state, the area is a fun place for kids to blow off some steam in between shopping in Les Halles (see page 100) or on the rue Montorgueil market street (see page 62). The first of the new playground structures will run along rue Berger.

Jardin des Tuileries

Rue de Rivoli, 1st arr. (Enter from Place de la Concorde, rue de
Rivoli, quai des Tuileries, avenue du Général Lemonnier, or
Passerelle Solférino.)

M Tuileries, Concorde

www.louvre.fr/en; select *Collection & Louvre Palace, Curatorial
Departments*, then *The Tuileries and Carousel Gardens*.

Daily 7am–9pm (summer); 7:30am–7:30pm (winter)

Free (except attractions noted below)

The Tuileries Garden is Paris's oldest public garden. Its name comes
from the *tuileries*, or tile manufacturers, that occupied the area
centuries ago. One of the best parks for children of all ages, the
Tuileries is located just minutes from the Louvre and is central to

many of Paris's major sights. The children's attractions, grouped along the Rivoli side of the park, are easy to find. Four **café-restaurants** and several ice cream stands for **snacks** are open within the park (see page 60). Pay **toilets** are located near the gates at the Concorde entrance and downstairs on the Rivoli side of the park near the children's attractions.

The Louvre borders one end of the Tuileries garden with Place de la Concorde at the other. The Orangerie and Jeu de Paume museums face each other on opposite sides of the park within the gardens near the Place de la Concorde entrance. The Orangerie houses some of Monet's famous water lily (*les Nymphéas*) paintings while the Jeu de Paume, of minimal interest to kids, exhibits 19th- to 21st-century photographs. If emerging from the Métro at Concorde, take a minute to enjoy the stunning view of the square, its obelisk, and the Eiffel Tower in the distance. The Luxor obelisk was a gift from Egypt in 1829; more than 3,000 years old, it is Paris's oldest monument. Older children may be interested to know that a guillotine was set up here during the French Revolution—more than 1,100, including royalty and ordinary citizens, were executed.

The rue de Rivoli side of the park near the Grand Bassin, the fountain closest to the Place de la Concorde entrance, is a kids' wonderland with trampolines, a carousel, pony rides (2,5€ for 5 minutes), model sailboat rental, and a sizable and engaging playground.

In mid- to late summer La Fête Foraine du Jardin des Tuileries (www.feteforaine-jardindestuileries.com) carnival sets up approximately 60 classic, charming (in an amusement park sort of way) rides that include a 19th-century carousel and the carnival's well-known Ferris wheel as well as food stands and game booths. Although it's fair food, the stalls are worth a look; carnival goers eagerly line up for a taste of roasted chicken, French cheeses, crêpes, waffles, *pommes d'amour* (candy apples), and other French classics.

Trampolines

Daily 11am–7:30pm, but opening time may vary
2€ for one 5-minute ticket or 15€ for 10 tickets
The trampolines are eight individual quadrants where kids ages 2 to 12 can jump in 5-minute turns. Lines will be long during school holidays and on Wednesday afternoons when French schools have half days. If the wait is long and you suspect 5 minutes won't be enough for your child, give the manager two tickets for a 10-minute turn.

Carousel

Rue de Rivoli side, between the Grand Bassin and the park
entrance near Tuileries Métro
Daily 11am–7:30pm
2,5€ per ticket; discount if 10 are purchased

Kids will love a turn on the vintage carousel. Cotton candy (*la barbe à papa*, or "papa's beard") and other sweets are sold at the carousel's ticket booth.

Playground

Rue de Rivoli side, between the Grand Bassin and the park
entrance near Tuileries Métro
Daily 7am–9pm (summer); 7:30am–7:30pm (winter)

The park's large playground has several sections: one for 3- to 12-year-olds, another for 6- to 12-year-olds, and a soaring play structure for 7- to 12-year-olds. It's well-equipped with hammocks, jumping pads with springs, rocking riders, and monkey bars. Parents who need a break will find benches along the edges of the playground and chairs under the wide metal canopy at one end of the park.

Musée de l'Orangerie

Jardin des Tuileries, quai des Tuileries side, near Place de la
Concorde entrance
01.44.77.80.07
www.musee-orangerie.fr
Daily 9am–6pm except Tuesday; closed May 1 and December 25
Guided tours in English Monday and Thursday at 2:30pm
Adult 7,5€; 25 and under free; free for all on the first Sunday of
every month
Audio guides in English 5€

Monet's water lily (*nymphéas*) paintings are displayed in this light, bright, and relatively small museum. Its size and the art make it accessible to families with young ones, many of whom may recognize the paintings. Eight impressively sized canvases fill the walls of two spacious, white rooms. Take an interactive 3D tour of the *nymphéas* rooms with your children on the museum's website before visiting.

Visitors are directed by a small sign to Keep Silent when entering the rooms, but it's only moderately quiet inside; even spirited young children should be fine. Tourists seem to bottleneck in the first room in peak tourist season, but there is plenty of open space in the second. The museum also houses a collection of works by Picasso, Matisse, Modigliani, and Cézanne.

Workshops for 5- to 12-year-olds are offered in French on Wednesdays when school-aged children are released early from school (approximately 2 hours, 7€). Many of the classes feature engaging, hands-on activities that might make them suitable for an adventurous child. In the Peindre comme Monet (Paint Like Monet) workshop for 8- to 12-year-olds, children observe Monet's paintings, learn about his techniques, and have a chance to paint their own inspired work.

There are four proper **cafés** in the Tuileries. The setting in this royal garden is luxurious—each is organized similarly with outdoor seating shaded by umbrellas and ancient, sprawling trees; several have a handful of tables located inside the bar/kitchen structure. All four restaurants are open daily during the garden hours: 7am–9pm (summer); 7:30am–7:30pm (winter).

Café Renard

Seine-side, near the Concorde entrance
01.42.96.50.56
www.caferenard.fr

Renard has been open since 1905; its French brasserie menu features champagne and aperitifs, as well as non-alcoholic cocktails; salads such as warmed goat cheese, seafood, and Niçoise; grilled sandwiches, steak, pasta, cheeses, ice cream, waffles, and crêpes. Parents can enjoy a beautiful Parisian setting while their kids have the option to venture out culinarily or stick with the familiar—the children's menu has a choice of chicken nuggets or a hot dog, fries, and ice cream (8,9€).

Café Reale

Rivoli-side, near the Concorde entrance
01.42.96.63.03
www.cafereale.eu

Classic Sicilian cuisine—antipasti, salads, pizza, and pasta—is served at this café managed by the Musée du Louvre restaurant group. A few tables are available inside but the space is too confining with young children. The kid's menu, served from noon–3:30pm for those under 12, has a choice of pizza or penne with

Bolognese sauce, ice cream or fruit salad, and a drink (8,5€). The menu is available in English, both online and at the café.

La Terrasse de Pomone

Seine-side, near the Louvre entrance to the gardens
01.42.61.22.14
www.terrassedepomone.fr

All of the seats at this café are on the terrace and have an excellent view of the Louvre Palace. Brasserie-style meals as well as a good selection of sandwiches, salads, savory tarts and crêpes, and lengthy dessert offerings including ice cream, waffles, fresh fruit salad, clafoutis, crème brulée, and other traditional French standbys are featured on the menu. For children 10 years and younger, there's pasta with ham and a choice of ice cream or crêpe (8,5€). From April 15–October 15 the café has an ice cream cart in the park.

Café Diane

Rivoli-side, near the Louvre entrance
01.42.96.81.12
www.louvre.fr/en/le-cafe-diane

Café Diane's menu has savory tarts, sandwiches, fresh fruit juices, and desserts to eat on the terrace or to take away (4,9€–8€). Café Diane also has an ice cream cart in the park.

Amorino

Near the Grand Bassin, Concorde-side entrance
www.amorino.com

This kiosk run by the French gelato chain comes in handy on hot days (see page 220, 314).

Jardin du Palais-Royale

6, rue de Montpensier, 1st arr.

01.47.03.92.16

M Palais Royal-Musée du Louvre

palais-royal.monuments-nationaux.fr/en

Sunrise to sunset

Free

Children can run and jump to their heart's content amidst the 260 black-and-white-striped columns of varying heights that fill the main courtyard of the Palais-Royal Gardens. *Les Colonnes de Buren*, named after the artist Daniel Buren who created them, were controversial when they were installed but have become a beloved part of the Parisian landscape. The columns provide a unique setting for a game of tag or hide-and-seek.

Shade trees flank this lovely, formal garden. Lawns are off-limits (*pelouse interdit*) but the park's gravel paths may inspire an unbridled sprint from kids. Parents will find plenty of benches, chic boutiques under the arcades, and a handful of **cafés** at the northern end of the gardens. Before leaving the courtyard gardens through the exit that leads to rue Vivienne, be sure to stop in or at least peek through the windows of the celebrated music box store Boîtes à Musiques Anna Joliet (see page 97).

Le Marché rue Montorgueil

Rue de Turbigo to rue Réaumur, 2nd arr.

M Les Halles, Étienne Marcel, Sentier

Tuesday–Saturday 10 am to 6 pm; Sunday morning

Now situated in the suburbs, Paris's wholesale market district had been located around Les Halles since the 12th century. A vestige remains, however—the neighborhood's permanent market street and a local favorite, rue Montorgueil. It is a superb introduction to outdoor markets and a quintessentially French cultural experience. Montorgueil has a decidedly authentic feel about it and it's geographically concentrated so easy to navigate with children. Locals come to take care of daily shopping and to socialize in the lively cafés and restaurants.

Several of the stores' façades date from the 19th century and are worth a look. Pâtisserie Stohrer at #51 is Paris's oldest bakery and remains one of its most cherished. Founded in 1730, the bakery is known for making the first baba au rhum pastry. Le Rocher de Cancale at #78 and Escargot de Montorgueil at #38, with its enormous golden snail that children love, are both well-preserved 19th–century storefronts.

Musée du Louvre

Rue de Rivoli, 1st arr.
01.40.20.53.17
M Palais Royal-Musée du Louvre
www.louvre.fr
Daily 9am–6pm; Wednesday and Friday until 10pm; closed Tuesday, December 25, January 1, and May 1
Adults 10€; free for under 18 years; free to all on the first Sunday of the month
Multimedia guides with commentary are available at rental desks near the entrance of each wing (adults 6€; under 18 years 2€).

Iconic, intimidating, and requisite, the Louvre is the museum to see. The age of your children will determine the length of the visit — toddlers are the most difficult to manage in this space. A child of 3½ to 4 years can last around 90 minutes in my experience, especially when you've worked to inspire interest beforehand.

We were only 35 minutes into our last Louvre visit when my 3-year-old daughter made her sixth request to go home. At that same moment we stepped into the Egyptian galleries. She took one glance at a sarcophagus and caught her second wind; her enthusiasm was irrepressible. Prep them, entice them, visit the bathroom before you head up to the galleries — and you will enjoy your visit to the Louvre *en famille*.

Even for adults, a visit to The Louvre is daunting; prepare yourself logistically and emotionally if you hope to tackle it with young ones. If you do manage to make it inside and see the art you've slated without major incident, consider the trip an overall success. Decide on a must-see list and check the Louvre website for more information. Nurture your child's interest by viewing pictures of the museum's collection online. For relatively ambitious planners, find a copy of *Objective Louvre* (Frédéric Morvan, English translation Jonathan Sly) or *A Kid's Guide to the Louvre for Adults* (Isabelle Bonithon Courant). Your best bet is to buy copies on line at: www.fnac.com, one of France's largest bookstores; even with international shipping, it is considerably less expensive than buying it in the U.S. Both books are filled with interesting, age-appropriate commentary that will make the Louvre more accessible to you and your children.

To avoid lines buy advance-purchase tickets: www.louvre.fr (on the English site, from the *Plan Your Visit* tab, choose *Online Tickets*).

Advance tickets have an unlimited date of validity and can be printed at home or mailed. Allow at least two weeks for the latter option; tickets cannot be picked up at the museum. Buying museum tickets from electronic machines is another expedient option that allows visitors to avoid the lines at the ticket windows; they are located under the pyramid and near the Restaurants du Monde food court in the Louvre's shopping mall.

The popular **Paris Museum Pass** allows entrance to more than 60 museums and monuments for either 2, 4, or 6 days (en.paris-museumpass.com). Admission is free for children under 18 in most museums, so they do not need a pass. Its benefits are mixed. The pace required to make it cost-effective is too hurried for children. Families, for example, would have to visit the Louvre, Musée d'Orsay,

Pompidou, and Musée Rodin in two days just to break even on the 2-day, 39€ pass. While they might not save money, pass holders will usually save time as they don't have to queue for tickets and are entitled to use designated entrances, separate from general admission, which see less traffic.

Choose your entrance wisely: the main entrance via the pyramid is excruciatingly busy, and once inside there is a second line to purchase an entrance ticket. The Porte des Lions off quai des Tuileries is probably the least crowded (9am–5:30pm, except Friday). The entrance from the Galérie du Carrousel at 99, rue de Rivoli is another good option, although visitors must pass through the underground shopping mall before heading into the museum's main hall (9am–10pm).

One of Paris's few luxury public **toilets**, the Point WC, is located near the mall's food court. There, parents will find a baby changing station, a private area for breastfeeding (a convenience virtually unheard of in France), and child-sized toilets (1,5€, www.pointwc.com). **Restrooms** with changing tables are also located behind the escalators of the Richelieu and Denon wings. The information desk in the Napoleon Hall handles loans of strollers and baby carriers (like Baby Bjorn) for use inside the museum (ID required; no charge). Escalators and elevators within the museum's galleries are indicated with a wheelchair symbol.

Workshops (*ateliers*) for children 4 to 13 years old are offered Wednesdays and Saturdays and daily during school vacations. The *ateliers* are conducted in French, but some of them, especially those for younger children that involve movement or hands-on art projects, may be enjoyable for non-francophones (the schedule and registration brochure is available in French only). Children attend classes with or without parents as specified in the schedule (available in pdf format at www.louvre.fr, the French site under the *Visites et Activités*, then *Ateliers adultes et enfants* tabs).

In the 2.5-hour workshop, Photographier le Louvre (Photographing the Louvre), 8- to 10-year-olds, accompanied by a parent, tour the museum with a professional photographer. Participants are loaned a camera as they visit and photograph selected works (13€, children 9€). The workshop Enfances, guides 4- to 6-year-olds to art that depicts children; it is followed by a hands-on visual art activity. Tickets can be bought up to two weeks in advance of the workshop or the same day. Call 01.40.20.51.77 (Monday–Friday 9am–4pm) or stop by the Acceuil des Groupes counter. Tickets are available for pickup 30 minutes prior to the activity.

To grossly simplify a visit to the Louvre, the three must-see works that make most adults' to-do lists are: the *Mona Lisa* (*La Joconde*), the *Venus de Milo* (*La Vénus de Milo*), and the *Winged Victory of Samothrace* (*La Victoire de Samothrace*). Knowing that these three pieces are the most frequented by tourists, the Louvre has posted individual direction signs guiding the way. Of course you won't be the first visitor to take a cursory tour of the museum, but with young children in tow you have an irreproachable reason for your brisk pace.

Two significant works that children often enjoy can be found in rooms adjacent to the Mona Lisa: *The Coronation of the Emperor Napoleon* (*Le Sacre de Napoléon*) and *Liberty Leading the People* (*Le 28 Juillet: La Liberté guidant le peuple*). A whirlwind tour of these five works can be done in 45 minutes when crowds are light. Plan extra time to negotiate the many stairs if using a stroller during your visit. In peak tourist season, the museum is best seen on a Wednesday or Friday evening after 6pm. An evening tour is also a brilliant option during the first jet-lagged days when your day begins in the afternoon. Family-friendly activities are rare after 7pm in Paris, so head to the Louvre.

Visit the works in this order: the *Mona Lisa*, *Winged Victory*, then *Venus de Milo*. It's an easy walk to the Egyptian antiquities section on this route if the kids are still willing. If you're feeling up to seeing all of the five works mentioned above, see the *Mona Lisa*, then walk past the *Mona Lisa* to the room on the left to see *Liberty Leading the People*. Head back to the *Mona Lisa*. Facing the *Mona Lisa*, head into the room on the right to see the *Coronation of Napoleon*. Facing the exit of this room, you will see *Winged Victory* sitting atop the large staircase. Head down the stairs and follow the indications to *Venus de Milo*. If the family agrees, walk to the nearby Egyptian galleries.

The Louvre's English website, www.louvre.fr, is an excellent planning resource. Under the *Activities and Tours* tab in the website's English version, select the *Visitor Trails* tab, then select *Children* in the search section. These child-centered, 1½-hour self-guided tours include: A Lion Hunt–French Sculptures, The Louvre–Outsize (a look at some of the largest works of art in the museum), and The Christmas Story. These step-by-step tours can be saved from the website and printed for convenience. They include historical information, a photo of each work to be visited, and clear directions to keep you on the right path.

Musée des Arts Décoratifs

107, rue de Rivoli, 1st arr.

01.44.55.59.25

M Palais Royal, Pyramides

www.ucad.fr

Tuesday–Sunday 11am–6pm; Thursday until 9pm; closed Monday

Adult 9€; free for under 18; audio guide included. Art workshops in French are available for children 4 years and older, through Ateliers du Carrousel: www.lesartsdecoratifs.fr/english-439/the-ateliers-du-carrousel.

Three museums are housed together in the Rohan and Marsan wings of the Louvre Palace. In addition to the Arts Décoratifs, the trio includes the Musée de la Mode et du Textile (fashion and textiles) and the Musée de la Publicité (advertising). Together they form one of the most important collections of design and decorative arts in the world.

The Musée des Arts Décoratifs celebrates artisanship at its finest, primarily through its display of furniture and decorative household items. The collection is organized chronologically and thematically. The 10 reconstructed period rooms that depict how the wealthy class in France lived from the late 1400s to the early 20th century have been popular with visitors since the museum opened in the 19th century.

With more than 12,000 toys in its collection, children will love the themed exhibitions in the Galerie des Jouets. The Galerie des Bijoux offers a look at stunning jewelry from medieval to modern times. Apart from the permanent collection, the museum hosts temporary exhibitions; the recent Petites & Grosses Bêtes considered the way animals, both real and mythological, have been rendered as toys from ancient to modern times. Les Histoires de Babar documented the stories of Babar in print and art; the museum also created several Babar-themed workshops for children to complement the visit. Designer Ralph Lauren loaned the museum 17 of the world's most prestigious sports cars from his personal collection, models rarely seen by the public, for the museum's immensely popular expo, L'art de l'automobile.

Restaurants du Monde

Mezzanine du Carrousel du Louvre, 1st arr.
99, rue de Rivoli
01.55.35.12.60
M Palais Royal-Musée du Louvre
www.restaurantsdumonde.fr
Daily 11:30am–8:30pm; Tuesday until 4:30pm unless otherwise noted

One of the most convenient options in the Louvre complex is Restaurants du Monde, a counter-service food court located on the mezzanine level of the shopping mall (the Carrousel du Louvre). Fast-food kitchens serve up international fare including Mediterranean, Middle Eastern, Spanish, Asian and Italian (Puro Gusto; daily 10am–8:30pm; Tuesday until 6pm). McDo, as it's called in France, is the ambassador of American cuisine, and usually has the longest lines (daily 10am–9pm; Tuesday until 8pm; McCafé—a separate espresso and pastry bar, daily 8am–7pm). Popular French gelato maker Amorino has a small stand at the Segafredo Zanetti counter (daily 7am–7pm; Tuesday until 4:30pm). The casual dining area is roomy, highchairs are available, and the variety of cuisines can be a refreshing change. Also nestled amid the shops of the Carrousel du Louvre is a busy Starbucks café.

Once inside the Musée du Louvre itself there are a number of options for snacks or a meal. **Café Richelieu** on the 1st (French) floor of the Richelieu wing and **Café Mollien** on the 1st (French) floor of the Denon wing both offer sandwiches, wraps, salads, and a warm daily special. **Café Richelieu** has a number of outside tables with a view of the pyramid. Up the escalators on the Richelieu mezzanine are the contemporary-styled cafeteria and self-service **Cafés de la Pyramide**, with reasonably priced daily specials such as curried and barbecued skewered meats, Basque chicken, pastas, and steamed fish (9€), and simpler fare such as pizza, quiche, and sandwiches. Menus for museum restaurants are available at: www.eliancemusees.com/UK/index.html.

Musée Grévin

10, boulevard Montmartre, 9th arr.
01.47.70.85.05
M Grands Boulevards
www.grevin.com
Monday–Friday 10am–6:30pm; Saturday–Sunday and holidays until 7pm; hours may vary, see website for exact opening times
Adults 22€; students 19€; 6–14 years 15€; under 6 free
Like most wax museums, Grévin is quirky, but it can be a fun and relatively quick detour for kids who have grown weary of seeing traditional art. Opened in 1882, Paris's wax museum offered the public a chance to "see" celebrities that they had only read about in newspapers. Today it exhibits around 300 figures, the majority of them

French personalities. A one-hour visit will allow ample time to tour the museum and take a few pictures with the wax figures. The Palais des Mirages, a light and music show included with admission, is popular with tourists, as are the beautiful, 19th-century rooms whose vintage décor has been preserved.

Opéra de Paris Garnier

Place de l'Opéra, 9th arr.

08.92.89.90.90

M Opéra

www.operadeparis.fr

Daily 10am–5pm; 10am–1pm on matinee performance days; closed
January 1, May 1, and when a special event is scheduled

Adults 9€; free for age 9 and under and one accompanying adult.
No credit cards.

Guided tours in English 11:30am and 2:30pm (July 10–August 31);
call 01.42.46.92.04 for up-to-date information.

Even young children are impressed by the size and opulence of
Charles Garnier's opera house—the grand marble staircase, floor-
to-ceiling gilt, majestic chandeliers, and the 2,200 sumptuous red

velvet seats. If they have any knowledge of the *Phantom of the Opera* story, they will probably ask to visit. Guided and self-guided tours are available. The guided visit, rather than a self-guided tour, offers greater access to the building as well as interesting trivia on the history and architecture of the Palais Garnier; visitors learn, among other things, that bees live on the roof of the opera house (their honey is sold at the nearby gourmet shop Fauchon) and that the structure sits above a maze of mysterious passageways. Guides keep tourists intrigued with the story of the deadly fall of the opera's great chandelier and tales of an underground pond and its resident oversized white catfish.

Be sure to check the performance schedule if you want to see the stunning main auditorium; most ticket agents won't remind you that during rehearsals it is closed to the public. For children who have previously attended and enjoyed a ballet or opera, a live show at the Opéra de Paris is unforgettable. If they haven't, the Palais Garnier is better enjoyed as a monument rather than a performance venue.

Paris L'Opentour
13, rue Auber, 9th arr.
01.42.66.56.56
M Havre-Caumartin, Opéra; RER: Auber
www.parislopentour.com
April 1–November 4, departs every 10 minutes daily 9:30am–8:30pm (Paris Grand Tour Route); November 5–April 1, departs every 30 minutes daily 9:40am–6:30pm (Paris Grand Tour Route)
1-day pass for adults 29€; 1- or 2-day pass for 4- to 11-year-olds 15€; 3 and under free
The open-bus, hop-on/hop-off tours have four different routes: the

Grand Tour, Montparnasse-St-Germain, Montmartre-Grands Boulevards, and Bastille-Bercy.

Hop-on-and-off bus tours are a mixed convenience. If you're on a short stay in Paris with two or more little ones in tow, it may be the only way to see many, if not all, of the city's major sights quickly and with minimal frustration—when the weather is clear and pleasant. If it rains, which it often does, riders bumble to the seats below; if the tour is crowded, you may find standing room only. The windows on the lower floor also make it difficult to get a good view of everything. Children are often lulled to sleep by the hum of the bus so families may end up doing more sitting and less hopping off than anticipated.

Paris Story

11 *bis*, rue Scribe, 9th arr.
01.42.66.62.06
M Opéra
www.paris-story.com
Daily 10am–6pm; film begins on the hour
Adults 10€; ages 6–18 years 6€; families (2 adults + 2 children) 26€

Paris Story condenses 2,000 years of French history into a 50-minute multimedia production. It traces the evolution of Paris from its earliest days as the Roman settlement Lutetia to modern times. It's touristy, but offers a quick introduction to French cultural and political history that can help visitors plan their visit or contextualize what they've already seen. The commentary, delivered in a choice of 14 languages, is heard through headphones, making the experience better suited to older children. Kids will also enjoy Paris Miniature, an interactive 3D-model of the city at table height, that features information, via touch screens, about 156 of Paris's most important monuments and sights.

Tour Jean Sans Peur

20, rue Étienne Marcel, 2nd arr.

01.40.26.20.28

M Étienne Marcel

www.tourjeansanspeur.com

Wednesday and weekends 1:30–6pm (early November–March);
Wednesday–Sunday 1:30–6pm (April–early November)

Adults 5€, children and students 3€

Brochure in English for children is available; best for children ages 7 and older.

This medieval structure is Paris's only fortified tower and the singular vestige from the palace of the Dukes of Burgundy, where Jean Sans Peur (John the Fearless), who became the de facto ruler of France from 1409–1413, eventually took refuge after having his first cousin and heir to the throne, Louis d'Orléans, murdered in 1407.

On their way up the 140 steps, visitors pass several installations decorated with chicken-wire mannequins dressed in period costumes. In addition to these curious scenes, the private toilet inside the tower usually piques a child's interest. It's the oldest in the city, dating to the 15th century when John the Fearless occupied the splendid palace. His WC sits at the top of the tower where his royal matter plunged a steep, 25-meter drop into a stone-lined septic pit. In his bathroom, the Duke of Burgundy enjoyed a padded seat, heating, and an air circulation system designed to reduce odors.

Each year the museum presents a themed exhibition based on medieval daily life. Past exhibits have featured hygiene, health, and school in the Middle Ages.

EAT

Also see Musée du Louvre, page 71.
Also see Jardin des Tuileries, page 55, 60.

Angelina

226, rue de Rivoli, 1st arr.
01.42.60.82.00
M Tuileries
www.angelina-paris.fr
Daily 9am–7pm

Opened in 1903, Angelina is *the* classic Parisian tearoom. Once a host to royalty and celebrities like George V and Coco Chanel, this turn-of-the-century salon de thé retains its luxurious décor and vintage ambience. It's a stop best suited for kids 7 years and older although if it's busy with tourists, the noise may be enough to muffle the voices of exuberant younger children. Angelina is famous for its signature Mont Blanc dessert, made with meringue, chestnut, and whipped cream (7,9€); the ultra-decadent, thick hot chocolate, Chocolat Angelina (7,2€), is equally celebrated, although the thick consistency may be too rich for some kids. If your children do have a chance to sample either, be prepared to head straight to the Tuileries where they can put their sugar-induced burst of energy to good use. Angelina also offers a varied menu with salads, traditional French main dishes, eggs cooked-to-order, fresh fruit salad, and juices (10€–13€).

Boco

3, rue Danielle Casanova, 1st arr.

01.42.61.17.67

M Pyramides

www.bocobio.com

Monday–Saturday 11am–10pm

Restaurateur Vincent Ferniot assembled five top-honored chefs to create a menu for his 100% organic, fast-food, eco-modern bistro, Boco. There are about 50 dine-in seats and a refrigerator with take-away items. If you're planning to eat in, it's best to avoid the 12:30–2pm lunch rush. The seasonal menu changes three times a year with a mix of salads and vegetable starters, main dishes (such as lasagna,

pasta with white sauce, vegetable tajine with couscous, chicken in a traditional cream sauce) and an excellent selection of desserts (chocolate mousse, rice pudding, crème caramel, and small cakes (3€–9€).

Boulangerie Julien

75, rue St-Honoré, 1st arr.
01.42.36.24.83
M Louvre-Rivoli
www.boulangerie-patisserie-artisanale-paris.com/index.html
Monday–Saturday 6:30am–8pm

Boulangerie Julien serves a variety of fresh sandwiches, pizzas, large salads, pastries, and yogurts to eat in or take away. Parents may be tempted by the carefully prepared Italian, chopped, and smoked salmon salads, rustic pizzas, or beautifully composed sweet and savory *verrines*. Seating is limited to a few barstools inside, but the terrace is roomy enough for strollers and children.

Boulangerie Régis Colin

53, rue Montmartre, 2nd arr.
01.42.36.02.80
M Sentier
Monday–Friday 5:30am–8pm

One street west of rue Montorgueil on relatively quiet rue Montmartre is Régis Colin, recipient of several prestigious baking awards that include Best Baguette in Paris, Best Croissant, and Best Galette des Rois. The pain au chocolat and the baguettes are particularly good as are the daily sandwich specials. A friendly staff greets the long line that forms during the weekday lunch rush that begins around 1pm. If you're hungry and in the neighborhood, it's worth a detour even if you have to wait.

Deliziefollie

7, rue Montorgueil, 2nd arr.
09.52.36.06.00
M Les Halles, Étienne Marcel
www.deliziefollie.eu
Daily noon–midnight

Pellegrino Gaeta, who received the International Award for Maîtres Glaciers, the top award for ice cream artisans, makes flavors like lemon meringue tart, pistachio, tiramisu, mojito, and chocolate-plum-armagnac at this unassuming *gelateria*.

Eric Kayser

33, rue Danielle Casanova, 1st arr.
01.42.97.59.29
M Opéra
maison-kayser.com
Monday–Saturday 7am–8:30pm

Given the scant seating inside, finding a spot here during the lunch-hour rush from 12:30–2pm is a nearly impossible feat, but this popular boulangerie has plenty of take-out picnic food if you're en route to the Tuileries. Fruit salad (3,5€), baguette sandwiches (6,4€), salads, juices, sodas, water, desserts, yogurt, and all kinds of breads are good choices for kids. Not to be missed: the white chocolate brioche, so incredible it's usually sold out after lunch (3€).
Additional locations: 8, and 14, rue Monge, 5th arr., **M** Maubert-Mutualité; 10, rue de l'Ancienne-Comédie, 6th arr., **M** Odéon; 18, rue du Bac, 7th arr., **M** Rue du Bac; 85, boulevard Malesherbes, 8th arr., **M** Saint-Augustin.

La Ferme

55–57, rue St-Roch, 1st arr.
01.40.20.12.12
M Pyramides
www.restolaferme.com/restaurants-la-ferme.php
Monday–Friday 8am–7pm; Saturday 9am–7pm; Sunday 10am–7pm

This casual, organic eatery has four locations in Paris. The self-service section is stacked with drinks, yogurt, cold salads, and sandwiches. Customers can order a set menu that includes a choice of hot daily specials, salad, and dessert (12€). The tomato, spinach, and goat cheese tourte is addictive, desserts and baked goods are scrumptious. Brunch is served on Sundays.

Additional locations: 28, boulevard de la Madeleine, 8th arr., **M** Madeleine; 33, rue de Berri, 8th arr., **M** Saint-Philippe-du-Roule.

Franprix

25–27, rue Montorgueil, 1st arr.

01.42.21.08.80

M Étienne-Marcel, Les Halles

www.franprix.fr

Tuesday–Saturday 8:30am–10pm; Sunday 9am–1pm

In addition to groceries, this small store south of rue Étienne Marcel stocks basic baby needs like diapers, wipes, baby food, and snacks.

Franprix

20, place du Marché St-Honoré, 1st arr.

01.47.03.01.42

M Pyramides

Monday–Saturday 9am–9pm; Sunday 9am–1pm

Next door to Le Pain Quotidien, this small branch of the well-known French grocery chain sells all of the essentials for baby: diapers, wipes, baby food, and formula. It's also a convenient stop to pick up snacks such as cookies or yogurt. Steps away, on place du Marché St-Honoré, a traditional open-air market with fresh vegetables, fruits, meats, fish, and clothing sets up Wednesday noon–8:30pm and Saturday 7am–3pm.

Galeries Lafayette Haussmann

40, boulevard Haussmann, 9th arr.

01.42.82.36.40

M Chaussée d'Antin-La Fayette

haussmann.galerieslafayette.com

Monday–Saturday 9:30am–8pm; Thursday until 9pm

Divided into three stores, the main Lafayette Coupole, Lafayette Homme, and Lafayette Maison, this sprawling department store complex has more than a dozen eating venues, nine of which are located in the main store. The best options for children are in the Coupole store. **Lafayette Organic** on the 3rd floor has a children's menu with a ham and cheese sandwich, apple sauce, juice, and a chocolate bar (9,9€). **Vue Sur Coupole** on the 2nd floor wows customers with an incredible view of the department store's ornate dome; it serves sandwiches, salads, and soup. **Le Lafayette Café** on the 6th floor has breakfast, a pasta-and-salad bar, and rotisserie-cooked meats. Children's clothing, toys, books, and gear is on the 5th floor along with baby-changing facilities.

Hard Rock Café

14, boulevard Montmartre, 9th arr.

01.53.24.60.00

M Grands Boulevards

www.hardrock.com/paris

Sunday–Thursday 8:30am–1am; Friday 8:30am–2am

A few doors down from the entrance to Passage Jouffroy is the Hard Rock Café. Paris's branch of this American chain offers continuous food service and a familiar menu. Children 10 and under can choose among a cheeseburger, pasta, chicken fingers, mac-and-cheese,

BBQ chicken drumsticks, and a roasted chicken salad, all served with fries or garlic toast and a drink (6,95€). The restaurant keeps busy with a mixed Parisian and international clientele; at peak times Hard Rock can be loud and the wait long. However, when hunger hits outside of traditional French eating hours (11:30am–2pm for lunch, 7–9:30pm for dinner), especially in the first few jet-lagged days, it's a good address to remember.

À la Mère de Famille

35, rue du Faubourg Montmartre, 9th arr.
01.47.70.83.69
M Le Peletier
www.lameredefamille.com
Monday–Saturday 9:30am–8pm; Sunday 10am–1pm

One of Paris's oldest sweet shops, À la Mère de Famille's signature bold, dark green storefront with gold lettering is easy to spot. The boutique was founded in 1761 — yes, 1761 — at this location on the corner of rue du Faubourg Montmartre and rue Richet and can be reached via Passage Verdot. Its elegant interior, decorated with delicate crystal pendant lights, mirrors the prettiness of the candies themselves: chocolates, nougats, *dragées*, and *pavée des fruits*. The store goes all out with its lovely window decorations during the winter holidays. À la Mère de Famille also has boutiques in the more genteel districts throughout the city including the 2nd, 6th, 7th, and 16th arrondissements, but they lack the architectural charm of the original location.

Alison Harris

Alison Harris

Alison Harris

Alison Harris

Monoprix Opéra

21, avenue de l'Opéra, 1st arr.

01.42.61.78.08

M Pyramides

www.monoprix.fr

Monday–Friday 9am–10pm; Saturday 9am–9pm

This busy location of the ubiquitous Monoprix chain has a grocery store with many take-away options. This branch also has a sizable infant and children's clothing department and baby care section.

Oh Mon Cake!

154, rue St-Honoré, 1st arr.

01.42.60.31.84

M Louvre-Rivoli

www.ohmoncake.fr

Daily 11:30am–8:30pm

Five minutes from the Louvre is a coffee shop-bakery that serves up seasonally inspired, salads, soups, savory tarts, and sandwiches. Lovingly prepared sweets are the draw: cupcakes, whoopie pies, fruit tarts, cookies, *choux à la crème* (cream puffs), and, of course, cakes.

Le Pain Quotidien

18, place du Marché St-Honoré, 1st arr.

01.42.96.31.70

M Tuileries

lepainquotidien.com

Monday to Sunday 8am–10pm

Le Pain Quotidien specializes in organic breads and uses almost entirely *bio* (organic) ingredients. This location of the familiar

Belgian chain serves up virtually the same menu as its international counterparts, including those in the U.S. Salads, sweet and savory tarts, *tartines* (open-faced sandwiches), and familiar breakfast items such as croissants and scrambled eggs provide something appealing for each family member. The interior of this location is too small for strollers or children; the terrace, however, provides ample space, except during the uncomfortably busy weekday lunch hour, around its perimeter.

Au Père Tranquille

16, rue Pierre Lescot, 1st arr.
01.45.08.00.34
M Les Halles, Étienne Marcel
Daily 9am–midnight, with continuous food service

This classic bistro has been open since the 19th century. Friendly service and a large terrace that wraps around the corner of rue Pierre Lescot and rue des Prêcheurs make it an appealing choice for families. If the weather isn't cooperating, the two floors of seating inside provide lots of room. It's a standard bistro menu — sandwiches, omelets, crêpes, outstanding salads, a *plat du jour*, and a kids' menu with a choice of hot dog or slice of ham, both served with french fries (6,5€). Still, Au Père is not a touristy spot; excellent food, continuous hours, and a sublime people-watching location keep it popular with locals.

A Priori Thé

35, Galerie Vivienne, 2nd arr.

01.42.97.48.75

M Bourse

www.apriorithe.com

Monday–Friday 9am–6pm; Saturday 9am–6:30pm; Sunday 12:30–6:30pm

Inside Galerie Vivienne, the intimate restaurant A Priori Thé embodies all of the character of the covered passages and offers plenty of

room for strollers and children on its terrace. The café's interior is rather quiet, but outside, the bustle from the gallery minimizes the sound of playful kids — and there's space for them to walk around. The lunch menu has a few safe bets for picky palates: roasted chicken, potatoes, and vegetables; the delicious, homemade pastries delight children and their parents alike around 4pm, during the French snack hour.

Le Valentin

32, Passage Jouffroy, 9th arr.
01.47.70.88.50
M Richelieu-Drouot, Grands Boulevards
www.le-valentin.fr
Daily 8am–7pm

Le Valentin is a cozy tea salon, pastry and candy shop that drips with vintage character. Located next to the wax museum Musée Grévin in a lovely 19th-century arcade, it's a charming spot to eat or grab a sweet snack and relax. Le Valentin's owner hails from Lorraine and recreates his region's favorites: *mirabelles de Lorraine* (tiny candied plums filled with marzipan), the *Damoiseau* (a blueberry cake made with almonds and honey), as well as the French classics. Le Valentin is typically good for breakfast: fresh orange juice, choice of tea or coffee, pain au chocolat or two mini-croissants, butter, and home-made jam (10€). The kitchen makes more than 20 homemade fruit preserves including La Favorite d'Henry IV, based on the king's favorite recipe. Lunch items are available to eat in or take away: salads, a club sandwich, quiche, desserts, and beverages.

Water Bar Colette

inside Colette
213, rue St-Honoré, 1st arr.
01.55.35.33.90
M Tuileries, Pyramides
www.colette.fr
Monday–Saturday 11am–7pm

This internationally known, trendsetting concept shop enjoys a cultish following that spans the entire spectrum of celebrity from fashionistas to athletes. Colette sells a little bit of everything from

Courtesy of Colette

everywhere and its creative directors have a knack for finding the coolest in up-and-coming local talent. A constant stream of visitors with an eye for the cutting-edge pours over Colette's eclectic selection of books, music, hi-tech gadgets, fashion, perfume, and other *objets*. There's no official children's section in the store, but the displays are stocked with eye candy for little ones: alien dolls, plush animals and figurines, kids' watches, toys, sunglasses, books, clothes, and a fun selection of other novelties.

Its basement houses the Water Bar, where bright blue chairs and polka-dotted tables encircled by a gallery wall make it a novel stop for older kids. The Water Bar has more than 50 bottled waters—still, sparkling, and flower-infused varieties—as well as sodas and fruit juices. The menu changes frequently but child-friendly options such as vegetarian lasagna, omelets, and club sandwiches (12€–17,5€) are always available. The menu can be found on Colette's website, under the *Now* tab, then *Water-bar* tab.

SHOP

Abis

24, Galerie Vivienne, 2nd arr.

M Bourse

01.42.96.54.76

abis.magasins-paris.com

Tuesday–Saturday 11am–2pm, 3–6:30pm

Souvenirs

A fun, kitschy shop with lots of unique souvenirs for children, tweens, and adults, Ibis stocks totes and purses made from French-designed fabric, pouches of all sizes decorated with French words and expressions, scarves, inexpensive jewelry, and cardboard stand-ups of fancifully-colored and patterned Eiffel Towers. Abis's friendly owner, Agnès, helps visitors navigate the shop (in French and English) with helpful advice on the perfect gift or souvenir.

Agnès b. Bébé et Enfant

2, rue du Jour, 1st arr.

Tél: 01.40.39.96.88

M Les Halles (Porte du Jour exit from Forum des Halles)

europe.agnesb.com

Monday–Saturday 10am–7pm (winter); 10:30am–7:30pm (summer)

Clothes & Accessories

The iconic Agnès b. opened her first boutique next door to the current shop in 1975. Now, her stores offering clothing for men, women, and children, as well as travel accessories, quietly occupy most of the retail space along rue du Jour. Gently, and without great fanfare, her company has grown to include hundreds of international boutiques, and she continues to personally design the brand's clothing. Fabrics are practical, playground-comfortable, and known for durability. Inspired by history and cinema, her casual yet chic style conveys authenticity. Most items are made in France, which keeps the prices in line with those of other designer boutiques.

Béaba

33, avenue de l'Opéra, 2nd arr.
01.44.50.53.15
M Pyramides
www.beaba.com
Monday–Saturday 10am–7:30pm
Baby Gear
Designer Jean-Michel Chaudeurge, who created Beaba's much-praised flagship product, the Babycook baby-food maker (a steamer-cooker-blender), notes that while the Babycook is sold internationally, the company's full product line is harder to track down. No longer—in Paris at least. In 2009 Beaba opened its only retail boutique in the world here at the corner of rue Danielle

Courtesy of Béaba

Casanova and avenue de l'Opéra. The colorful, ergonomic baby products neatly contrast against the boutique's bright, white interior: think baby nursery meets modern art gallery with a fun, eco-conscious edge. The company's entire range of products — high chairs, bottle warmers, baby monitors, bouncers, diaper bags, baby utensils and dishes, pacifiers, potty-training seats, and lily-pad-shaped bath thermometers are on display.

La Boîte à Joujoux

41–43, Passage Jouffroy, 9th arr.
01.48.24.58.37
M Richelieu-Drouot, Grands Boulevards
www.joujoux.com
Monday–Saturday 10am–7pm
Toys, Collectibles

A vast inventory of miniatures for dollhouse enthusiasts — make that fanatics — with everything from miniscule Persian rugs to Beauty and the Beast-style candelabras and 12-volt crystal chandeliers is stocked in this Passage Jouffroy shop.

Boîtes à Musique-Anna Joliet

9, rue de Beaujolais, 1st arr.
01.42.96.55.13
M Palais Royal-Musée du Louvre, Bourse
Monday–Saturday 10am–7pm
www.boitesamusiqueannajoliet.com
Music Boxes

Specializing in music boxes, this tiny shop located at the northern end of the Palais-Royal garden, sells all types of melody makers from plain musical mechanisms to the most elaborate boxes decorated with carousels, birds, dancers, teddy bears, and hot air balloons (35€–6000€).

Brentano's

37, avenue de l'Opéra, 9th arr.
09.62.62.58.95
M Opéra
Monday–Saturday 10am–7:30pm
Books

There are more postcards and souvenirs than books here; still, there's a mid-sized selection of children's books in English as well as kids' bilingual French-English vocabulary books in this recently renovated historic bookshop.

La Droguerie

9 and 11, rue du Jour, 1st arr.
01.45.08.93.27
M Les Halles (Porte du Jour exit from Forum des Halles)
www.ladroguerie.com
Monday 2–6:45pm; Tuesday–Saturday 10:30am–6:45pm; hours may vary in August
Fabric/Crafts

La Droguerie is a veritable cave of wonders for the knitting or craft enthusiast. The boutique resembles a vintage drugstore; apothecary shelves sparkle with hundreds of glass jars of beads, buttons, and every imaginable embellishment. It also stocks a spectrum of gorgeous yarns and fabrics. Original patterns for sewing and knitting children's clothes, some in English, are displayed throughout. Craft

Pia Jane Bijkerk

Pia Jane Bijkerk

Pia Jane Bijkerk

Pia Jane Bijkerk

kits in neat, tidy boxes, assembled with pre-cut fabrics, include everything needed to make decorative animals, baby booties, and other whimsical objects. Kids and adults, especially those who enjoy arts and crafts, will swoon over La Droguerie's selection.

Le Forum des Halles

101, Porte Berger, 1st arr.
01.44.76.96.56
M Les Halles; RER: Châtelet-Les Halles
www.forumdeshalles.com
Monday–Saturday 10am–8pm
Clothes, Accessories, Toys, Décor, Food

Parisian teenagers flock to this shopping complex and the area that surrounds it, which makes it a fun spot for your teens to observe fashion and cultural trends among their own age group. Shoppers will find a wide variety of relatively inexpensive stores within the mall and in the aboveground boutiques that border the Forum along rue Rambuteau and other nearby streets. France's largest clothing and accessory chains are scattered throughout the shopping mall: Catimini, Petit Bateau, Okaïdi, and Du Pareil au Même (see page 257). The full list of shops can be seen at www.forumdeshalles.com, under the *Enfants* then *Mode Enfants* tabs.

The shopping mall will remain open during the extensive renovation of the area, scheduled for completion in 2016. The areas of the Forum of most interest to parents are located on Level -3. An Espace Bébé equipped with changing table, an area for breast-feeding, and a spot to warm baby food is located near Porte Rambuteau, Level -3. Stroller rental (10am–8pm) is offered at the Points Accueil for Portes Lescot and Rambuteau, Level -3. The mall's **restrooms** are also on the same level, next to the pedestrian entrance of the Parking Porte Rambuteau and Porte Berger (0,50€).

There is a wide choice of casual, quick-service **food venues** on Level -3 including Quick, McDonald's, La Croissanterie, La Brioche Dorée, Bretzel Love, Pomme de Pain, Viagio Pasta Café, Pastavino, Starbucks, and Nolita Caffe.

Okaïbi-Okaïdi

Forum des Halles, level -2, Porte Lescot, 1st arr.
01.40.26.55.41
www.okaidi.fr
Monday–Saturday 10am–8pm
Clothes

Styles at Okaïdi are ultra-basic, at times uninspired, but come at a lower price point than most French brands. Okaïdi fits 2- to 14-year-olds while its sister-store, Okaïbi, offers lines for 0- to 5-year-old boys and girls. There are a total of nine stores in the city—some locations also sell shoes, baby gear, feeding accessories, and layette basics. ID Group, the brand's parent company, owns the high-end Jacadi label as well (see page 103).

Catimini

Forum des Halles, Level -1, Porte Lescot, 1st arr.

01.45.08.51.34

www.catimini.com

Monday–Saturday 10am–8pm

Clothes

Catimini's designs are marked by bold colors and playful prints. The brand has five Parisian stores and three retail points within Galeries Lafayette Haussmann and Montparnasse and Printemps Haussmann as well as boutiques throughout the world.

Apache

Forum des Halles, Level -2, Porte Rambuteau, 1st arr.

01.44.88.52.00

www.apache.fr

Monday–Saturday 10am–8pm

Toys, Baby Gear, Sporting Goods

This branch of the French toy chain sells sporting gear — skateboards, mini skateboards, scooters, and helmets — as well as sandbox toys, kites, hula hoops, and outdoor games. Apache features toy brands such as Lego, Corolle, Playmobil, and a variety of characters: Hello Kitty, Barbie, Littlest Pet Shop, and Barbapapa. For unique and useful souvenirs, check out the backpacks and lunch boxes.

Jacadi

1, boulevard des Capucines, 2nd arr.
01.44.51.76.41
M Opéra
www.jacadi.com
Monday–Saturday 10am–7:30pm
Clothes, Shoes

The elegant look of Jacadi has caught on internationally and boutiques can now be found on five continents. In Paris there are 14 branches with four more locations inside various Printemps department stores. Jacadi's clothing fits children 0–12 years old; a special line, Mademoiselle Jacadi, is designed for young girls 10–14.

Librairie Galignani

224, rue de Rivoli, 1st arr.
01.42.60.76.07
M Tuileries
www.galignani.com
Monday–Saturday 10am–7pm
English Books

The Galignani family opened the first English bookstore on the European continent in 1801 in Paris; in 1856 it was moved to its present location on rue de Rivoli. This refined shop has a superb selection of English-language kids' books, including coloring books, about the capital and its monuments.

Au Nain Bleu

5, boulevard Malesherbes, 8th arr.

01.42.65.20.00

M Madeleine, Concorde

boutique.aunainbleu.com

Monday 2–7pm; Tuesday–Saturday 10am–7pm

Toys

Founded in 1836, Au Nain Bleu is Paris's oldest, and one of the world's fanciest, toy shops. For many, the name is synonymous with Parisian chic and luxury. From the beginning, the shop's handmade, customized toys and extravagant doll clothes were popular with Europe's rich and royal. The flagship product, a made-to-order teddy bear, still hand-sewn in France, is a chance to bring a piece of idealized Paris home. Customers who can't visit the store in person can customize a teddy online—its size, color, ribbon, eye color, an optional interior music box or embroidered name—and have it shipped to them (from 66€ for the 8-inch size to 460€ for a 32-inch bear; shipping to the U.S. approximately 16€). Move over Cinderella: Au Nain Bleu also sells elaborately detailed princess costumes including Empress Josephine, Marie Antoinette, and Marquise de Trianon gowns. There are plenty of shelves with offerings for the *sans culottes*, too: makeup sets, wooden toys, loads of stuffed animals, and comparatively less expensive international toy brands such as Lego.

Not So Big

38, rue de Tiquetonne, 2nd arr.
01.42.33.34.26
M Étienne Marcel
www.notsobig.fr
Monday–Saturday 11am–7:30pm
Clothes, Accessories, Toys

When the multi-brand boutique Not So Big opened in 2002, it was the first concept store in Paris to focus specifically on kids' and baby items. It's a favorite among French celebrity moms like fashion icon Inès de la Fressange, the former face of Chanel and author of several how-to Parisian style guides, and for Parisians who want chic baby fashion, décor, and toys. Not So Big created its own clothing label for kids in 2003. The aesthetic is lighthearted, at times edgy — onesies printed with pictures and embroidered with French expressions are some of their most popular items. Not So Big carries a host of other independent labels including Bobo Choses from Spain, WoWo, and the Asian-inspired French brand Hakka Kids. The Montorgueil-neighborhood shop is also packed with novel toys — French magnetic poetry words, wooden puzzles, coloring books, and pacifiers and bottles with tattoo-style images. There's a nursery furniture section — what's not on display in the store can be ordered. Not So Big also sells unique décor pieces for older kids' rooms such as the Bauhaus-inspired, primary-colored Bauchair, decoupaged birdhouses, and wall-mounted animal sculptures.

Alison Harris

Pain d'Épices

29, 31, 33, Passage Jouffroy, 9th arr.
01.47.70.08.68
M Grands Boulevards
Monday 12:30–7pm; Tuesday–Saturday 10am–7pm
www.paindepices.fr
Toys

Pain d'Épices is an old-fashioned wonderland of toys, costumes, crafts, stuffed animals, and dollhouse miniatures that fills two levels. On the ground floor are miniature typewriters, flowerpots, lamps, and everything imaginable to embellish, decorate, or build a dream dollhouse. The adjacent room has an exhaustive selection of delight-

Alison Harris

Alison Harris

ful *doudous* ("lovies") from Moulin Roty. Upstairs is another exciting maze stacked with puzzles, stickers, hand puppets, and other toys.

Si Tu Veux (jouer)

68, Galerie Vivienne, 2nd arr.
01.42.60.59.97
M Bourse
situveuxjouer.com
Monday–Saturday 10:30am–7pm
Toys

Filled with goodies for children, Si Tu Veux is a tranquil store with a vintage vibe that fits in well with the rest of lovely Galerie Vivienne. The shelves are stocked with Haba and other wooden toys, arts and crafts kits and dozens of stocking-stuffer-sized toys such as whoopie cushions, rubber balls, and wind-up toys. There's also a good selection of kids' books in French.

WH Smith

248, rue de Rivoli, 1st arr.
01.44.77.88.99
M Concorde, Tuileries
www.whsmith.fr
Monday–Saturday 9am–7pm; Sunday and bank holidays 12:30–7pm
English Books

WH Smith is Paris's largest English bookshop. Its mega-sized section of kids' books upstairs is packed with fiction and non-fiction titles as well as a selection of English books about France and Paris. (There's also a candy aisle filled with American- and British-brand sweets.) Each Wednesday at 3:30pm during the school year the store hosts Kids' Club, a reading in English for children ages 4–9 (rsvp required, see website for information).

Village Joué Club

Passage des Princes
5, boulevard des Italiens, 9th arr.
M Richelieu-Drouot
01.53.45.41.41
www.villagejoueclub.com
Monday–Saturday 10am–7:30pm
Toys

Village Joué Club is a group of toy shops that occupy over 21,000 square feet in the Passage des Princes, making it Paris's biggest toy store—it's actually one department store split into 10 different retail spaces. There is a shop each for wooden toys, educational games, infant toys, puzzles and board games, dolls, model building, Legos, and party supplies, as well as a children's hair salon and a space for birthday parties. You'll find mainly corporate brands and characters here; independent boutiques will have a more unique selection.

Zef

32, rue de Richelieu, 1st arr.
01.42.60.61.04
M Quatre Septembre, Bourse
www.zef.eu
Monday–Saturday 10:30am–7:30pm
Clothes & Accessories

Zef designs clothes for children 0 to 18 years old. A variety of conservative as well as more playful colors and prints characterize Zef's cool, modern style. The color palette is *très* Parisian—black, white, gray, blue, and a bit of red here and there. You will pay designer prices, but expect fine quality; a chic tunic or blouse for girls is around 65€, sweatshirts for boys 45€. Zef also sells children's linens—and don't forget the shoes reminiscent of some of France's most iconic styles: ballerina flats, espadrilles with a slight wedge, and the *sandales lavandou* that evoke the spirit of K Jacques's strappy leather St. Tropez-chic sandals. The brand recently opened its online store and has a handful of boutiques in the city including Ciao Bella, a shop with fashions for girls 12- to 18-years-old.

Additional locations: 15, rue Debelleyme, 3rd arr., **M** St-Sébastien-Froissart; 55 *bis*, rue des St-Pères, 6th arr., **M** St-Germain-des-Prés; Zef—Ciao Bella, 14, rue du Pré aux Clercs, 7th arr., **M** Rue du Bac; 93, avenue Kléber, 16th arr., **M** Trocadéro.

STAY

Hôtel Brighton

218, rue de Rivoli, 1st arr.

01.47.03.61.61

M Tuileries

www.paris-hotel-brighton.com

Average double: from €249

Across from the Tuileries Garden, 4-star Hotel Brighton oozes Old World character. Nineteenth-century décor — soft colors, paintings in gilded frames, and period furniture — creates a pleasant ambience. The location is stellar, nestled in among the elegant luxury shops and hotels along rue de Rivoli. Families have quite a few options — at a comfortable 300–400 square feet, Superior rooms (from 240€) can accommodate up to three people; extra beds for children under 10 and baby beds are complimentary. Suites and the larger executive rooms sleep three adults or two adults and two children under 12 (from 305–345€). The hotel has rooms with doors facing each other in a small, private hallway but they don't connect internally. At 19€, the buffet breakfast is steep but tasty, as is the 16€ continental breakfast served in-room, but there are many nearby cafés that serve breakfast.

Hôtel Chopin

46, Passage Jouffroy, 2nd arr.
01.47.70.58.10
M Richelieu-Drouot, Grands Boulevards
www.hotelchopin.fr.
Average double: from 98€

This simple, clean 2-star hotel at the end of Passage Jouffroy is a charming option for small families on a modest budget. Located in the Grands Boulevards neighborhood, it's about a 10-minute walk north of Palais-Royal. Portraits of Georges Sand and Frédéric Chopin hang on either side of the lobby's antique upright grand piano; the hotel's romantic décor evokes a bygone era. Budget rooms can be exceptionally dark, so opt for the Classic which are small, but adequate for up to three people (136€). There's no air-conditioning or Wi-Fi, but a tiny elevator is available to take guests up to rooms on the 3rd floor and above, which offer better views than the lower floors.

Hôtel du Louvre

Place André Malraux, 1st arr.
01.44.58.38.38
M Palais Royal-Musée du Louvre
www.hoteldulouvre.com
Average double: from 280€

Paris's first palace hotel sits in an enviable location, facing the Louvre museum. This 5-star hotel works for smaller families (Deluxe rooms for two adults and one child up to age 12) or for those whose families occupy two or more rooms; for the latter, a 50% discount is offered on additional rooms. At around 400 square feet and larger, the junior suites and suites are spacious for Paris. Hôtel du Louvre retains its vintage charm; some rooms can be tired, but overall the staff is accommodating and the location is prime.

Hôtel Relais du Louvre

19, rue des Prêtres St-Germain l'Auxerrois, 1st arr.
01.40.41.96.42
M Louvre-Rivoli, Pont Neuf
www.relais-du-louvre-paris.com
Average double: from 218€

Housed in an 18th-century building, this hotel is just steps from the Louvre and equally close to the Île de la Cité and Notre-Dame. Families have several choices: triples, two generously sized junior suites for four, and a large 645-square-foot apartment, complete with a small kitchen, for families of five (from 218€, 285€, and 455€ respectively). Rooms on the hotel's courtyard side are bigger than those on the street side—two of them have a third bed. Connecting rooms are also available. Its 21 spotless rooms, attentive staff, and brilliant location make Hôtel Relais du Louvre a great choice for families.

PLAY

EAT

Marais & Bastille

PLAY

Balabus
Gare de Lyon, 20 boulevard Diderot, 12th arr.
M Gare de Lyon
www.ratp.fr/en/ratp/c_22257/balabus
Sunday afternoons and holidays from April to September
A regular Métro or bus ticket may be used; adults 1,70€; 4–10 years: ,85€; under 4 free

This bus tour by public transit is operated by the city of Paris and stops at most of the city's principal tourist sights. It's included in the Paris Visite transportation pass (good for 1, 2, 3, or 5 consecutive days—purchase online or at a Métro ticket window; adults from 9,75€; 4–11 years 4,85€) and also may be accessed with a regular Métro or bus ticket. The route takes travelers between Gare de Lyon and La Défense and lasts approximately one hour without any stop-offs.

Bois de Vincennes
12th arr.
M Porte Dorée, Château de Vincennes
www.paris.fr/English

One of Paris's largest parks is located just outside of the *peripherique*, the auto route that marks the boundary between Paris and its suburbs. The Bois de Vincennes, however, is owned by the city and considered part of its 12th arrondissement. Given its distance from central Paris and the number of activities available here, plan to spend a full day. These woods offer the perfect respite from the noise, traffic, and activity in the city. There are limitless possibilities for activities with children within the expansive green space: pony rides, marionette theaters, boat rental, carousels, a working farm, and several fun playgrounds. There are five **restaurants**, seven **snack bars**, and picnic spots throughout the park. The Parc Floral de Paris, a vast botanical garden-cum-playground located inside of the Bois de Vincennes, is a destination in and of itself with a miniature golf course, rides, swings, tunnels, ping-pong tables, concerts, and magic and puppet shows.

BOIS DE VINCENNES

Parc Floral de Paris

118, Route de la Pyramide, 12th arr.

01.43.28.41.59

M Château de Vincennes

www.paris.fr/english

Daily 9am–8pm (April–September); 5pm (winter months), 6pm (February), 7pm (March)

Free from late September–early June; adults 5€, 7–26 years 2,5€, under 7 years free; also free during Les Pestacles festival on Wednesdays from June to mid-September. The same entrance fee is charged on weekends during this time period and on days with performances.

Just beyond the enormous, 14th-century royal palace, the Château de Vincennes, is this pleasant, fun-filled botanical garden. Children can see the metamorphosis of butterflies in Le Jardin des Papillons (butterfly garden) from mid-May to the end of September and observe countless species of plants and flowers. There's an elaborate playground and more than 50 activities, some with a fee, including miniature golf played around a course of Paris's most famous monuments, an electric train, a ball pit, zip line, and pedal cars.

The Parc Floral hosts the Paris Jazz Festival (www.parisjazzfestival.fr) with free concerts in June and July. Les Pestacles (www.lespestacles.fr), a series of child-themed, Wednesday afternoon concerts and activities, opens in June and continues through late September.

Les Marionnettes du Parc Floral de Paris
Near Parc Floral main entrance off Esplanade St-Louis
01.49.23.94.37
M Château de Vincennes
www.guignolparcfloral.com
Wednesday, Saturday, Sunday 3pm and 4pm while school is in session; daily 3pm and 4pm during school vacations; daily, except Monday, 3pm, 4pm, 5pm in July and August. 2,8€ per person; children must be 2½ years or older to attend.
Check the theater's official website for current show titles and photos.

Pony rides, Lac Daumesnil
M Porte Dorée
Wednesday noon–7pm; Saturday, Sunday, and holidays 10am–7pm; school vacations 10:30am–7pm (weather permitting)
¼ hour 7€, ½ hour 12,5€

Pony rides, Lac de St-Mandé

M Saint-Mandé

www.animaponey.com

Wednesday, Saturday, Sunday, and vacations 3–6pm (weather permitting)

3€ per child

Maximum weight for children 66 lbs.

Théâtre des Marionnettes de Paris

Orée du Bois de Vincennes (behind the Mairie de St-Mandé [City Hall], near the carousels)

06.75.23.45.89

M Saint-Mandé

www.lesmarionnettesdeparis.com

Wednesday, Saturday, Sunday 3:30pm and 4:30pm when school is in session; daily 3:30pm and 4:30pm during school vacations; hours vary in summer, see website.

Children 3 and older 3,5€

Approximately 10 different puppet shows are performed throughout the year; recent features include The Fox and the Hen, Little Red Riding Clown, and The Magic Beans.

Boat rental

Lac Daumesnil

01.43.28.19.20

M Porte Dorée

Daily 9:30am–8pm; last rental at 7pm

10,8€ per hour for 1–2 people; 11,8€ per hour for 3–4 people

Boat rental
Lac des Minimes
06.86.08.01.12
M Château de Vincennes
March–November: opens at 1:30pm Wednesday and Saturday,
11am Sunday; open daily during school vacations; closed in winter
9€ per hour for 1–2 people; 11€ per hour for 3–4 people

Carousels
There are a number of merry-go-rounds in the Bois de Vincennes;
three are clustered around Lac de St-Mandé (**M** Saint-Mandé)
and two near Lac Daumesnil (**M** Porte Dorée). 11am–7:30pm,
2,5€

La Ferme de Paris
1, route du Pesage, 12th arr. (facing the Hippodrome)
M Château de Vincennes
01.71.28.50.56
Holidays and weekends 1:30–6:30 pm, April–September; 5:30pm
October and March; 5pm November–February
Free
This working educational farm inside le Bois de Vincennes
gives children and visitors a hands-on introduction to farm life.
It's tucked into the southern part of the park, a 35-minute walk
from the Château de Vincennes Métro station. The experience is
designed to help kids make the connection between the farm and
their dinner plate—to better appreciate the origin of what they
consume each day. Around 4pm, visitors are invited to help feed
the animals—cows, rabbits, goats, sheep, pigs, and chickens—
or assist with other seasonal jobs.

Canauxrama

Boarding point varies between Porte de l'Arsenal and Bassin de la Villette depending on the day; check website for the current schedule.

01.42.39.15.00

M Bastille

www.canauxrama.com

Cruises begin at 9:45am and 2:30pm year round

Adults 16€; students and seniors 12€ (not valid on weekends and holidays); children 4–12 8,5€; 3 and under free (reduced rates for tickets purchased online: 13,5€/8€)

Boat tours along the Canal St-Martin are organized daily by Canauxrama. These are scenic excursions off tourist-trodden paths that older children may enjoy—at 2½ hours, they are too long for little ones. Travelers see a quieter side of Paris as they pass gently under a canopy of shade trees and through the arches of old-fashioned pedestrian bridges. If the area looks familiar, you may remember Amélie Poulain skipping stones into Canal St-Martin at one of the locks in the film's opening sequence. Kids will delight in watching the waters swirl and in feeling the sensation of water levels rise and descend as the boats pass through the locks along the route.

Centre Georges Pompidou

Place Georges Pompidou, 4th arr.
01.44.78.12.33
M Hôtel de Ville or Rambuteau
www.centrepompidou.fr
Wednesday–Monday 11am–9pm; closed Tuesday; Galerie des Enfants 11am–7pm
Adults 12€; 18–25 years 9€; free for under 18
English tours of the collections each Sunday at noon. Audio guides with long, short (45 minutes), or children's commentary are available at the entrance (5€/4€; under 13 years free).
Europe's largest collection of modern art is housed within Centre Georges Pompidou, also known as the Beaubourg. Children love the museum's quirky façade with its bold, primary colors and exposed ductwork. All sorts of street performers—musicians, fire-eaters, jugglers, magicians—engage and entertain pedestrians in the plaza in front of the building. In fact, my family found the façade and the action outside the museum to be more appealing than touring the artwork inside, but it may have been the mood of the moment.

Inside the museum, on Level 0, is La Galerie des Enfants, an interactive exhibition space for children that provides a dynamic, child-

centered initiation into modern and contemporary art. One section is for children 2 to 5 years old, another for kids 6 to 12. Hands-on workshops and guided visits in French for 2- to 12-year-olds (adult and child duo: 10€) are held Wednesdays, Saturdays, and Sundays and daily during school vacations at 3pm. Depending on the activity, some may be appropriate despite a language barrier. On the first Sunday of each month when admission to the museum is free, an art workshop is offered to families free of charge; a list is available in French at www.centrepompidou.fr/enfants.

The collection of work on Level 5 features some well-known artworks created between 1905 and 1960. Among the exhibits are paintings by Matisse, Picasso, Miró, Kandinsky, Mondrian, Rothko, Pollock, and several stunning Calder mobiles. Kids may find these works particularly appealing.

The best options for eating inside Centre Pompidou include **Café Mezzanine** on Level 1 and, on the second, **Cafétéria de la Bpi**, a more casual self-service venue. From its vantage on the sixth level of the Centre Pompidou, **Restaurant Georges** offers an unforgettable view of Paris. Soak it in over a drink on the terrace, but enjoy your meal elsewhere as prices can be quite high.

Children will enjoy the vividly painted modern art sculptures by Niki de Saint Phalle in the nearby Stravinsky Fountain next to Centre Pompidou off of rue St-Merri. The fountain features 16 moving (and spraying) mechanical sculptures inspired by Stravinsky's major works.

Cimitière du Père Lachaise

Père Lachaise Cemetery
16, rue du Repos, 20th arr.
01.55.25.82.10
M Père Lachaise or Philippe Auguste
www.paris.fr/english
March 16–November 5: Monday–Friday 8am–6pm, Saturday 8:30am–6pm, Sunday 9am–6pm; November 6–March 15: opening hours are the same, closing at 5:30pm.

Older teens like to make the trek out to this cemetery filled with some of western culture's most famous names. Chopin, Colette, Abélard and Héloïse, Jim Morrison, Oscar Wilde, and Molière rest amidst 70,000 other graves. A pdf map of Père Lachaise can be found under the *Visit* tab at the listed website; it indicates the location of over 150 of the most requested sites within the cemetery. Although Père Lachaise is considered a tourist destination by many, it is a cemetery. Remind your children to keep their voices down and to be respectful—or the guards will be happy to tell them for you.

Cirque d'Hiver Bouglione

110, rue Amelot, 11th arr.
01.47.00.28.81
M Filles du Calvaire
Saturday and Sunday, 2pm and 5:15pm (late October to early March). Weekday schedule varies but show times remain 2pm and 5:15pm. See website; dates change annually.
Adults 26,5€–56,5€ (reservation required); 3 and under free

The Cirque d'Hiver is one of Paris's most entertaining spectacles. Owned and operated for decades by the Bouglione family, the

2-hour performances dazzle audiences with all of the classic acts: clowns, daring trapeze artists, performing elephants, prancing horses, and trained tigers. The richly decorated theater, inaugurated in 1852, seats 2,000 visitors around a single ring. The Bougliones have built a circus empire throughout Europe and are known for the quality and innovation of their acts. The *cirque* can be great fun even for those who typically are not fans of such spectacles; kids will watch from the edge of their seats as they enjoy a show that has delighted generations.

Le Double Fond

1, place du Marché Ste-Catherine, 4th arr.
01.42.71.40.20
M St-Paul
www.doublefond.com
One-hour, child-oriented magic show Wednesday, Saturday, Sunday at 4:30pm
Ages 5–11, 10€

On the postcard-perfect place du Marché Ste-Catherine is a one-of-a-kind café-magic theater. Situated north of rue St-Antoine, between rue de Sevigné and rue de Turenne, this secluded square can be tough to find. The father-daughter team of Dominique and Alexandra Duvivier, joined by a small supporting cast of magicians, has run this show for more than 20 years. One-hour performances geared towards children and their families are held on Wednesdays and weekends (followed by an optional workshop, both in French). Kids will enjoy the simple, yet masterfully performed classic magic tricks. The theater itself is nothing fancy, but for magic enthusiasts, it's still a fun diversion.

Hôtel de Ville

1, place de l'Hôtel de Ville, 4th arr.

01.42.76.43.43

M Hôtel de Ville

www.paris.fr

(Weather permitting) Monday–Friday noon–10pm; Saturday, Sunday, holidays 9am–10pm (check website for exact dates/times each season)

Free for those with their own skates. Skate rental: European sizes 25–49 (U.S. kids' size 8–adult size 16½) 5€ and a valid ID; children's double bladed skates, size 27 (U.S. 9½) and smaller, free. Gloves required.

For more than a decade, from mid-December to mid-February, the main plaza in front of Paris's city hall, the Hôtel de Ville, has been transformed into an open-air ice-skating rink. Twinkling holiday lights reflecting off of the ice create an unforgettable, sparkling spectacle. The enormous rink is divided into two sections — a large space for adults and children who are comfortable skating, and a smaller, separate area for young children. Animal-shaped push-chairs are provided for kids to help them keep their balance as they shuffle around the ice.

Jardin de l'Arsenal

53, boulevard de la Bastille, 12th arr.

M Bastille or Quai de la Rapée

Daily 8am–11pm

The stroll through the Jardin de l'Arsenal, a lushly planted, terraced garden that runs along boulevard de la Bastille, is enchanting. Visitors walk past colorful boats and yachts docked in the Bassin de

l'Arsenal (Arsenal Boat Basin). The basin, known also as the Port de l'Arsenal, accommodates up to 230 recreational boats. It connects the Seine with Canal St-Martin, which begins at place de la Bastille. It's also a boarding point for Canauxrama, a tour company that runs cruises along Paris's canals and the Seine river (see page 122).

Near rue Jules César is a footbridge (and a public **toilet**) that crosses to boulevard Bourdon on the other side of the water. There are two nautically themed, well-equipped playgrounds in the immediate area, one for 2- to 8-year-olds, the other for 3- to 14-year-olds.

Le Marché Aligré

Place Aligré and rue Aligré, 12th arr.

M Ledru-Rollin

marchedaligre.free.fr

Tuesday–Saturday 8am–1:30pm; Sunday 8am–2:30pm; closed Monday

Marché Aligré is an outdoor market frequented primarily by residents of the surrounding neighborhoods. Known for its comparatively inexpensive prices and quality products, it's a perfect destination for budding foodies. There are two sections: the covered Marché Beauvau and the outdoor stalls that run along rue Aligré and fill the main plaza. The stalls sell everything from produce to household items to antiques to flowers. Marché Aligré is worth a stroll even if you're apprehensive about shopping in a market where it's unlikely the merchants speak English. Kids will like the colors, smells, street music, and the overall energy of the place.

Musée Carnavalet

23, rue de Sévigné, 3rd arr.

M Chemin Vert, St-Paul

01.44.59.58.58

carnavalet.paris.fr

Tuesday–Sunday 10am–6pm; closed Monday and holidays

Free for permanent collection

Musée Carnavalet details the history of Paris from prehistoric times to the present. Two mansions connect to house an encyclopedic collection of art, furniture, tableware, drawings, and photographs. Due to the number of exhibited items, a visit may be overwhelming for children, yet they may enjoy the glamour of the brightly colored

© DAC/A. Dumont/Courtesy of Musée Carnavalet

rooms—dazzling yellow, turquoise, and lilac—all with elaborately carved, gilded walls. Other highlights are the Neolithic canoes, dated to 4500 BC, and an ancient mammoth molar. Kids also seem to enjoy the gallery of exquisitely crafted shopkeepers' signs from the 16th to 20th centuries. There are signs from bakers, wig makers, wine sellers, insurance companies, inns, and one of the most interesting, from the Cabaret du Chat Noir, that depicts a frightened black cat with bulging yellow eyes standing inside of a crooked crescent moon. Audio guides with a 30-minute commentary designed for children are available in English (5€). The museum organizes themed walks for families and a variety of hands-on art workshops in French for kids ages 4 to 12. Information is available under the *Activities* tab on Musée Carnavalet's English website. The huge courtyard garden, while not a playground, provides needed roaming space and fresh air before or after a visit.

Musée de la Curiousité et de la Magie

11, rue St-Paul, 4th arr.

01.42.72.13.26

M St-Paul, Sully-Morland

www.museedelamagie.com

Wednesday, Saturday, Sunday 2–7pm

Adults 9€; children 3–12 years 7€

If you or your children are fascinated by magic and want a break from the typical tourist regime, this off-path, hands-on museum — with a magic show included — is an entertaining destination. Visitors descend a few steps into a world of eerie, vaulted rooms as a professional magician leads the way through a collection of historic props that includes magic trunks, hats, and wands. Children love the Hall of Mirrors, Gallery of Optical Illusions, and the live magic show at the end of the visit. Although the performance is in French, card tricks and the magician's sleight of hand need no translation. Workshops at the École de Magie (Magic School) teach basic tricks using cards, ropes, money, rings, cups, and balls. These two-hour, Saturday-afternoon classes are held throughout the year for adults and children 12 years and older (20€, in French).

Musée de la Poupée

Impasse Berthaud, 3rd arr.

01.42.72.73.11

M Châtelet-Les Halles, Rambuteau

www.museedelapoupeeparis.com

Tuesday–Sunday 10am–6pm; closed Monday and holidays

Adults 8€; 12–25 years 6€; 3–11 years 4€; free Sunday from 10am–noon for children under 12 years

More than 500 dolls are exhibited in this tiny museum, tucked away on a cul-de-sac near Centre Pompidou. Its permanent collection traces the history of doll making in France from 1800 to 1945. Although my daughters were giddy at seeing so many dolls in one place, my three-year-old quickly decided that glass and wooden dolls wouldn't be much fun to play with; she also chose to breeze past the displays of dolls with "creepy eyes," those with lifelike stares. Still, most girls will enjoy seeing the evolution in materials and changing aesthetics presented in the museum's displays. Each year Musée de la Poupée welcomes several temporary shows; recents included Barbie and Ken, Doll Houses, The Art of Miniature, and Regional Dolls from Europe.

Musée des Arts et Métiers

60, rue Réamur, 3rd arr.

01.53.01.82.00

M Arts et Métiers

www.arts-et-metiers.net

Tuesday–Sunday 10am–6pm, Thursday until 9:30pm; closed Monday

Adults 6,5€; students 4,5€; free for under 18

Three audio guides are available for adults and teenagers: a one-hour tour presents the 30 must-see items in the museum; a 2½-hour presentation describes 75 pieces; the Liberté tour allows visitors to select commentary on any display within the museum. The museum also has a 1½-hour audio guide, created especially for children 7 to 12 years old (5€ each audio guide).

Dedicated to *arts et métiers* (the arts and trades) and founded in 1794, this is Europe's oldest science and technology museum. It is organized around seven themes: scientific instruments, material, construction, communication, energy, machines, and transportation. Exhibits are grouped chronologically from pre-1750 to post-1950, and are easy to follow. Kids can see a number of seminal inventions here first-hand such as the first mechanical calculator and the first self-propelled vehicle. Ancient measuring tools, astronomical instruments, printing presses, and telegraphs are also on display. For science buffs the museum has a functioning example of Foucault's pendulum—as well as his original—and the equipment from the 18th-century lab of Antoine Lavoisier, the father of modern chemistry.

Le Musée des Arts et Métiers is best suited for children 7 years and older. For younger ones, the highlight will probably be the gallery of full-sized, historic aircraft and automobiles (including a Formula 1 race car), exhibited in the St-Martin-des-Champs abbey section of the museum.

Various workshops in French for children 4 to 12 years old are held throughout the week. Subjects have included the Lumière brothers, silly robots, the history of electricity, and the history of the bicycle. Children visit objects related to the theme, then create their own project. Check the website for the current schedule; reservations are required (adults 6,5€; children 4,5€).

Photo: Pavillons de Bercy

Three times a month, the automatons' theater highlights a few items from the museum's collection during a 45-minute show. These exquisitely crafted, 18th-, 19th- and 20th-century figures, both eerie and fascinating to watch, are set in motion with the turn of a key and tick along on their internal mechanisms; collection standouts include the Dulcimer Player (la Joueuse de Tympanon) owned by Marie Antoinette, and Fernand Martin's automated toys. See the museum's website under the *Visits and Activities* tab for dates.

Musée des Arts Forains

Pavillons de Bercy
53, avenue des Terroirs de France, 12th arr.
01.43.40.16.15
M Cour St-Émilion
www.arts-forains.com

Photo: Pavillons de Bercy

Adults 14€; under 12 years 5€

Open to the public for visits by reservation only. Reservations may be made by e-mail; see website for information.

Thousands of pieces from Jean-Paul Favand's private collection of fairground art and memorabilia are housed in this magical museum. Inside, visitors can ride the 19th-century bicycle carousel or play vintage carnival games. The museum's reservation process keeps away some travelers although it's seen more traffic since appearing in the film *Midnight in Paris*. It typically opens to the public with no need for a reservation for one week during the winter holidays and during Les Journées du Patrimoine (see Seasonal Events for Families, page 32).

Musée National Picasso

Hôtel Salé, 5, rue de Thorigny, 3rd arr.

01.42.71.25.21

M Chemin Vert or St-Paul

www.musee-picasso.fr

Wednesday–Monday, April–September 9:30am–6pm; until 5:30pm
November–March; closed Tuesday

The Picasso museum is closed for renovations until the summer
of 2013. It houses a vast collection of the artist's work; more than
500 works are displayed in what was once a private mansion in the
Marais, the Hôtel Salé. Kids will enjoy looking for Picasso's colorful
renderings of children: *Maya with Doll* (*Maya à la poupée*), *Paul as
Harlequin* (*Paul en arlequin*), and *Painter and child* (*Le Peintre et
l'enfant*) among others. His animal sculptures are another treat:
Chat (*Cat*), *La Chèvre* (*Goat*), and *La Petite Chouette* (*The Little Owl*).
Visits and workshops for children are offered in French; see the
museum's website for more information.

Place de la Bastille

2 *bis*, place de la Bastille, 11th arr.

M Bastille

Children who have a basic knowledge of French history may be curious to see the Bastille, even after assurances that all traces of the
prison are gone. Only a monument stands on the site — and it's a
monument commemorating the July Revolution of 1830. Around the
Colonne de Juillet is an enormous and intimidating traffic circle; it's
downright scary. If you're in the area, there are two convenient public *sanisettes*: one facing 41, boulevard Bourdon (place de la
Bastille), the other facing 4, boulevard Richard Lenoir. There is a
public lavatory at 5, place de la Bastille, M Bastille, St-Antoine exit.

Place des Vosges

30, place des Vosges, 4th arr.

M St-Paul, Chemin Vert

Monday–Friday 8am–sunset; Saturday–Sunday 9am–sunset

On sunny days, locals stretch out on the grass and enjoy the warmth in what many consider to be the most beautiful square in Paris. Red bricks and white stones placed in splendid symmetry, decorate the façades of the 36 attached homes that together form the oldest planned square in Paris, dating from the early 17th century. These regal town homes sit atop charming, stroll-worthy arcades lined with cafés, art galleries, and shops. Victor Hugo lived in Place des Vosges for 16 years; his home has been preserved as a museum at Maison de Victor Hugo (6, place des Vosges). There's a playground nearby for 1- to 12-year-olds with rocking animals, a jungle gym, a slide, and a hammock. In the center of the Place des Vosges, separate from the playground, is a sandbox. The closest **restroom** is a *sanisette* (automatic, self-cleaning toilet) near the St-Paul Métro station, 123, rue St-Antoine, 4th arr.

Promenade Plantée

From avenue Daumesnil, behind the Bastille, across the 12th arrondissement to the Bois de Vincennes at the edge of Paris, 11th arr.

M Bastille

www.paris.fr

Daily 9am–sunset; hours vary by month, see website

This lushly planted 4.5-km path follows an old railway line that once linked place de la Bastille with the Bois de Vincennes and Varenne-St-Maur, an outlying suburb. The meandering walkway, also called La Coulée Verte (the green belt), rises up atop the Viaduc des Arts along avenue Daumesnil; the elevation affords a unique view of Paris. The lovely brick arches below once supported an elevated railroad track; they now house art galleries and artisan workshops. If you're staying in the area, it's worth knowing about the promenade, but it's not worth a special trip. At times there are relatively long stretches without an obvious entrance/exit point, so it may not be the best stroll to take with a young or potty-training child.

The path descends and crosses through, at street level, the Jardin de Reuilly, a park with ponds and lawns for play and picnics; then passes an inviting playground for 2 to 14 year olds (15, rue Albinoni, 12th arr., **M** Montgallet). The promenade continues through another street-level park, Square Charles-Péguy, with play structures for 1- to 12-year-olds and public ping-pong tables (21, rue Rottembourg, 12th arr., **M** Michel Bizot).

Rollers & Coquillages

www.rollers-coquillages.org
Sunday 2:30 pm
Free

The rollerblading event known as Rollers & Coquillages takes place near place de la Bastille on Sunday afternoons. This organization of rollerblading enthusiasts has gathered each Sunday for more than 13 years for a 3-hour skating tour of Paris. Departure is at 2:30pm from place de la Bastille (in front of the store Nomades, 37, boulevard Bourdon). Participants typically number between 1,000 and 10,000 for this family-oriented activity, but at times have been as many as 29,000. Police keep the selected route traffic-free during the tour. The route changes weekly but always ends and begins at place de la Bastille. If you haven't brought your rollerblades along, no worries — Nomades rents them (6€ ½ day, 9€ full day, 150€ deposit). The skating tour is open to adults and children 7 and older; participants are welcome to join the tour for as little or as long as they wish. Check the website for the week's specific itinerary.

EAT

L'As du Fallafel
34, rue des Rosiers, 4th arr.
01.48.87.63.60
M St-Paul
Sunday–Thursday 11am–11:30pm; Friday until approximately 5pm;
closed Saturday.

There's almost always a long line at the take-away window in front
of this bright green restaurant. Try not to be discouraged; it moves
quickly, the staff is usually jovial and the food well worth the wait.
New York Times food writer and author Mark Bittman calls L'As du
Fallafel "the one culinary destination in town I never skip." While
most customers order their food to go, there are tables inside. The
dine-in menu features chicken kebabs, french fries, chicken sausage,
schwarma, and various falafel plates. With kids, however, the interior
of this Marais institution is just too loud and limited on space. The
alternative isn't much prettier; it's almost impossible to walk and
eat this messy meal. The best option is a few minutes away from the
restaurant—a lovely, little-known, hidden gem of a public garden,
Le Jardin Francs-Bourgeois-Rosiers. With benches and a small playground (for ages 2 to 6), it's an ideal spot to enjoy your meal. The
interior gardens of two private mansions will eventually be joined
together to complete the green space; the first phase, the current
park, was completed in 2007. As such, the garden is an enclave,
invisible from the street. Visitors enter through l'Hôtel de Coulanges,
which houses the Maison de l'Europe. A dark green plaque is posted
on the street entrance to the Hôtel indicating the garden's name.

Cross the courtyard, heading towards the left into the Hall de la Maison de l'Europe, continue through a pair of glass doors and *voilà*—the secret garden!

From l'As du Falafel, head in the direction of rue Vieille du Temple. Turn right on rue des Hospitalières St-Gervais, then right on rue des Francs-Bourgeois. Continue about 200 feet (70 meters) to #37. The opening hours of the park change frequently: 2–7pm until the daylight savings time change at the end of October; in winter 2–5:15pm; March 1 until the spring time change 2–6:30pm.

Berko

23, rue Rambuteau, 4th arr.
01.40.29.02.44
M Rambuteau
www.cupcakesberko.com
Tuesday–Sunday 11:30am–7:30pm

Looking for comfort food near Centre Pompidou? Berko specializes in cupcakes and cheesecakes made with Philadelphia Cream Cheese. Parisian cupcakes tend to be dry; Berko is one of the few bakeries in the city that seems to get the moist part right. Berko also serves mini-pastries and light lunch menus—salads, soups, bagels, and savory *tartes* with a side, drink, and dessert (9,5€–10,8€). Customers line up between two cases surrounded by sweets. Deliciously displayed cupcakes are on one side: salted butter caramel, white chocolate ganache-raspberry, Teddy Bear marshmallow, or rose-lychee-raspberry (2€ each, 10,8€ for 6). Decadent cheesecakes are arranged on the other side of the aisle, with pomme tatin, crème brulée, and praline noisette (4,3€–5,1€) among the flavors.

On weekends, the queue can stretch past the dozen or so seats and out the door of this small shop.

Additional location: 31, rue Lepic, 18th arr., **M** Abbesses or Blanche

Au Bistrot de la Place

2, place du Marché Ste-Catherine, 4th arr.
01.42.78.21.32
M St-Paul
Daily until 11pm

This pretty square, north of rue de Rivoli, is hidden away from the rush of Paris. The bistro's brown and orange awning covers a spacious terrace that is popular with neighborhood families. The tranquility of the square, continuous food service, and a kid-friendly menu—spaghetti Bolognese (12,5€), cheeseburger, fries, and a salad (15,5€)—make this the best choice for a snack or meal on Place du Marché Ste-Catherine. There are plenty of choices for parents looking for French fare as well: grilled fish, steak, roasted lamb, rabbit, cassoulet, mussels and fries, foie gras, pasta, and delicious desserts (prix fixe 18,5€–23€).

Breizh Café

109, rue Vieille du Temple, 3rd arr.
01.42.72.13.77
M Filles du Calvaire
www.breizhcafe.com
Wednesday–Sunday noon–11pm

Breton Bertrand Larcher brought his *crêperie* to Paris in 2007 by way of Japan and Brittany. Both the *galettes* (savory crêpes) and crêpes (sweet) made with organic buckwheat flour, artisanal butter, and traditional Breton buttermilk (*lait ribot*) are sublime. Children will like the *galettes* filled with ham and cheese or scrambled eggs or one of the many dessert crêpes (4€-19€). Also on the menu are artisan cheese and charcuterie platters and around 20 handcrafted ciders made from apples (*cidre*) and pears (*poiré*). The interior is light and inviting—a kind of Japan-meets-Brittany, modern aesthetic. It's child-friendly except during peak meal hours when it becomes too crowded for young children. At just two minutes from the Picasso museum, it's a useful address. Menus are tri-lingual (French, Japanese, and English); reservations are recommended.

L'Ébouillanté

6, rue des Barres, 4th arr.
01.42.74.70.52
M Pont Marie
ebouillante.pagesperso-orange.fr
Tuesday–Sunday noon–10pm

Tucked away on a tranquil pedestrian street near the Seine is one of Paris's most pleasant café terraces. The chairs and wobbly tables, shaded by the ancient church of St-Gervais-St-Protais, sprawl across both sides of the medieval cobbled passage. The café-tearoom has a light menu: omelets, savory tarts, copious salads, and delicious homemade sweets, but savory-filled crêpes, called *bricks*, are its specialty. The patio is packed by 1pm; plan to arrive early during the lunch hour. Behind the vibrant blue façade is a casual dining room. Art exhibitions are held upstairs on the café's first floor.

On and around rue des Barres are several of Paris's oldest houses. The timbered house at #12, a few doors down from l'Ebouillanté, dates from the 16th century and is now a youth hostel. A two-minute detour from the café at #11–13, rue du François Miron, are two timbered, medieval homes whose earliest construction dates to the 14th century.

Happy Days Diner
6–8, square Ste-Croix de la Bretonnerie, 4th arr.
01.42.77.69.34
M Hôtel de Ville
www.happydaysdiner.com
Daily 9am–midnight

Never underestimate the value of having an address with familiar food and all-day service. Happy Days Diner is located off of busy rue des Archives on square de St-Croix de la Bretonnerie. Inside, it looks and sounds like an American diner (except for the French waiters and clientele): black-and-white-checkered floors, bubblegum- and turquoise-colored seating, blaring 50s music, and vintage posters. The menu is in English and French and features various burgers (9–11€), hot dogs, salads such as a Caesar and a Cobb (12,5€), sundaes, decent milkshakes and fries, onion rings, and nachos. The restaurant is large enough for a stroller and young children, but gets loud during peak meal times. Of course it's not what you've come to Paris to eat, but with tasty, identifiable food, a fun atmosphere, and a clean restroom, it just might be the right place at the right time. Additional locations: 25, rue Francisque Gay, 6th arr., **M** St-Michel; 25, rue de la Reynie, 1st arr., **M** Châtelet.

Jacques Genin

133, rue de Turenne, 3rd arr.
01.45.77.29.01
M Filles du Calvaire
www.jacquesgenin.fr
Tuesday–Sunday 11am–7pm; Saturday until 8pm

Don't let the refined décor of this incredible chocolate and pastry shop deter you from stopping in with the kids for a *goûter*, as the locals do. Food writer and chef David Lebovitz, a longtime admirer of this master chocolatier, blogged that he was "completely wowed" by Genin's shop. Inside, tables are limited; plan to arrive before 4pm as they fill quickly. Genin's strawberry tarte was recently honored as one of the best in Paris, but he is equally admired for his éclairs and made-to-order millefeuilles and revered for his subtly flavored chocolates and caramels (pastries 6€–8€). The salon de thé serves espresso drinks, tea, hot chocolate, and fresh fruit juices.

Le Loir dans la Théière

3, rue des Rosiers, 4th arr.
01.42.72.90.61
M St-Paul
Daily 9:30am–7pm; tea after 3:30pm (customers are not obliged to order a meal)

This unassuming tearoom appears small from the exterior, but once inside it's spacious. The vibe is laid-back and bohemian—worn wood floors, antiques, vintage furniture, and walls covered in aged posters. It's a perfect place for an afternoon snack with children; if your kids will eat savory tartes, pasta, salads, or omelets, then lunch, thankfully, is also an option.

The café's name ("the dormouse in the teapot") and the dining room's large faded mural of *Alice in Wonderland* recalls Lewis Carroll's book. The seating is part living room — soft, squishy, vintage armchairs and sofas around coffee tables — and part café, with tables, chairs, and a comfortable banquette along the wall. The savory tarte selection changes daily; it may be eggplant, olive, and tomato, or goat cheese with shallots, both served with a salad (8,5€). Personal computers are not allowed inside the café; le Loir is a place for conversation. For Paris, it's almost noisy at lunchtime; for parents it's comfortably animated, well suited to energetic toddlers and children. The desserts are exquisite — don't miss the *tarte au citron meringuée* (lemon meringue tart) topped with a billowy, 6-inch layer of Italian meringue (6,5€).

Maria Luisa

2, rue Marie-et-Louise, 10th arr.
01.44.84.04.01
M Goncourt, République
Maria Luisa, Facebook page
Monday – Thursday noon – 2:30pm, 8 – 11pm; Friday – Saturday 7:30 – 11:30pm; Sunday until 10:30pm
Young families arrive at noon in force to fill the terrace at Maria Luisa. Fresh ingredients and a light, crispy crust baked in a wood-burning oven make this Canal St-Martin-area pizzeria one of the best in Paris. The menu is basic — red and white pies with simple toppings, pastas, salads, calzones, and Italian desserts (10€ – 15€ for pizzas, 9€ child's menu).

Page 35

4, rue Parc Royal, 3rd arr.

01.44.54.35.35

M St-Paul

www.restaurant-page35.com

Tuesday–Friday 11:30am–3pm, 7–11pm; Saturday–Sunday continuous service from 11:30am to 11pm; hours vary in August, see website

Crêpes with Salidou, a rich caramel sauce made with salted butter and crème fraîche from Quiberon in Brittany, are the house specialty at Page 35 (7,5€). There are plenty of tantalizing combinations on the dessert menu including crêpes with caramelized apples, Salidou, and vanilla ice cream flamed with Calvados or a tropical-inspired crêpe flambée with pineapple, Salidou, mango sorbet, and rum. The lunch menu is a rare value in this neighborhood of museums (Picasso, Cognacq-Jay, Carnavalet); mains feature savory crêpes, cod, chicken, pasta, or more traditional dishes such as boeuf bourguignon and confit de canard (two courses: 11,9€, three courses 13,9€). The crêpes, both savory and sweet, are consistently delicious; other selections on the menu can be hit or miss. Tables are tightly squeezed in this restaurant/crêperie/salon de thé, so avoid the lunch rush.

Across the street from the restaurant is Square Léopold Achille, 5, rue du Parc Royal. It's a lovely park, bordered with benches, and with a central sandbox and playground for 2- to 6-year-olds.

Du Pain et des Idées

34, rue Yves Toudic, 10th arr.
01.42.40.44.52
M Jacques Bonsergent
www.dupainetdesidees.com
Monday–Friday 6:45am–8pm

One of Paris's top bakeries is just minutes from Canal St-Martin. Du Pain et des Idées is a traditional boulangerie that serves artisanal breads, *viennoiseries*—croissants, brioche, pain au chocolat—and seasonal fruit tartes; you won't find pastries here. In 2008, Gault & Millau honored the owner, Christophe Vasseur, as Paris's Baker of the Year. Vasseur says bakers in his shop use their hands more than

machines; it takes seven hours to create a baguette here, while the typical Parisian bakery spends only 90 minutes. The building itself is a beautifully restored vintage *boulangerie* dating from 1889. Specialties include the *chausson à la pomme fraîche* (a turnover made with fresh apples, as opposed to the applesauce most bakeries use), La Mouna (a brioche flavored with orange blossom), and Pain des Amis (a thickly crusted flatbread with a nutty flavor). Stop in for a snack before or after strolling along the canal.

Parce que!

26, avenue Daumesnil, 12th arr.
09.53.85.64.63
M Bastille, Ledru-Rollin
www.parceque-paris12.fr
Monday–Friday 9am–5pm

Looking for a picnic lunch to take to the Promenade Plantée? Parce que! is a busy, inexpensive self-service eatery that faces a section of the Viaduc des Arts, the complex of art galleries and artisan shops located under the Promenade Plantée. All of the food is made each morning on site, is additive- and preservative-free, and organic when possible, with an emphasis on local and seasonal ingredients. The café's eco-friendly containers make take-out a cinch. There's also a small terrace and space to eat inside. The menu offers home-made savory tarts, soups, pastas, salads, sandwiches, and desserts (3,5€–7€; lunch menus from 7,3€).

Pause Café Bastille

41, rue Charonne, 11th arr.
01.48.06.80.33
M Bastille, Ledru-Rollin
Monday–Saturday 8am–2am, Sunday 9am–8pm

Local hipsters and families fill this lively café on the corner of rue Keller and rue de Charonne. The interior is bright with citrus-colored chairs, mosaic tiled floors, and an inviting terrace painted in play-room colors. Menu choices for kids include pasta, risotto, cheese-burgers, fried rice, juices, handsome pastries, and daily specials (3–12€). The interior has lots of room for strollers and roaming kids; the banquette that runs the length of one of the walls is ideal for corralling active infants or toddlers. Pause Café's staff is friendly but service is extra-slow at times; brave the waiter's probable dismay and ask for your check well before you need it.

Les Philosophes

28, rue Vieille du Temple, 4th arr.
01.48.87.49.64
M Hôtel de Ville, St-Paul
Daily 9am–2am with continuous service

Les Philosophes café is ideally situated on the corner of busy rue Vieille du Temple and the tranquil rue du Trésor. The foot traffic on rue Vieille du Temple is a welcome distraction for children. Rue du Trésor is a pedestrian street so if the kids get antsy it's a picturesque stroll—or run—up and down its cobblestones. The café's large terrace also gives families room to stretch. Its seasonal menu focuses on locally sourced, organic-whenever-possible produce. Children may find the scrambled eggs (*œufs brouillés*) (7€), sautéed potatoes (4€), charcuterie platter (11€), *tartine* with organic jam (3€), and the fresh fruit salad (7,5€) appealing. Meals are simple and fresh and while lengthy, the menu sticks to the basics like salads and grilled sandwiches. It also includes more than 70 choices for wine. The café's continuous service may be useful during the first jet-lagged days.

Pink Flamingo

67, rue Bichat, 10th arr.

01.42.02.31.70

M Jacques Bonsergent

www.pinkflamingopizza.com

Tuesday–Saturday noon–3pm and 7–11:30pm; Sunday continuous
service noon–11:30pm

The "pink nik" — pizza delivery to the banks of Canal St-Martin — is
the truly original concept behind this popular pizzeria owned and
operated by a Franco-American couple. Order at the restaurant
counter and take your pink balloon (and drinks) to the canal, just
three minutes away on foot. Relax and enjoy the idyllic spot; 15 minutes later your pizza arrives via bicycle delivery. The pizzas, made
with organic flour and locally sourced ingredients, with imaginative

names like L'Almodovar (with paella toppings), La Che (topped with Cuban-style pork and plantains), L'Obama (bacon and pineapple chutney), or the simple La Dante (tomatoes, basil, and mozzarella) have become a neighborhood staple (10,5€–16€). If a canal picnic isn't in the cards for your family, the restaurant has a small dining room.

Additional locations: Pink Flamingo Marais, 105, rue Vieille du Temple, 3rd arr., **M** St-Sébastien-Froissart or Chemin Vert (delivery available to the Jardin de l'Hôtel de Salé park and playground across the street from the restaurant and behind the Picasso museum). There are two more locations in Paris's 12th and 18th arrondissements; see website.

Courtesy of Pink Flamingo

Courtesy of Pink Flamingo

Popelini

29, rue Debelleyme, 3rd arr.
01.44.61.31.44
M Filles du Calvaire
www.popelini.com
Monday–Saturday 11am–7:30pm; Sunday 10am–3pm

This tiny pastry boutique is named for the Italian chef in Catherine de Medici's court credited with the creation of *choux à la crème*, or cream puffs. Each day 10 flavors, including coffee, dark chocolate, pistachio, lemon, Earl Grey, salted-butter caramel, rose-raspberry, and a seasonally inspired *chou du jour* are neatly arranged in colorful rows (1,85€ for one; 11€ for six; 2,8€ *chou du jour*). Kids will love the playfulness of these little treats.

Rose Bakery 2

30, rue Debelleyme, 3rd arr.
01.49.96.54.01
M Filles du Calvaire, Arts et Métiers
Tuesday–Sunday 9am–5:30pm; food served noon–4pm, Sunday from 11am

The emphasis here is on organic. Without a sign outside indicating its name, the restaurant can be hard to find, but this hasn't hindered business—it's usually packed. This is one of the few places in Paris to serve gluten-free baked goods. Sunday brunch is a thing of beauty, ordered à la carte with choices such as scrambled eggs, pancakes with maple syrup, homemade granola, pizzettes, artisanal sausage, fruit salad, savory tartes, scones, burgers, and vegetable platters (6€–15€). Service can be slow and impersonal but local families still enjoy Rose Bakery 2. Arrive as early as possible for brunch to avoid prohibitive wait times.

SHOP

Antik Batik

18, rue de Turenne, 4th arr.

01.44.78.02.00

M St-Paul

www.antikbatik.fr

Monday 12:30–7:30pm; Tuesday–Sunday 10:30am–7:30pm

Clothes

Antik Batik is known for the exoticism of its adult hippie-chic styles. The collections reflect the designer's distant travels. Made in locations such as Nepal, India, and Indonesia, natural fabrics are colored and embellished using artisanal methods like batik, crochet, and embroidery. The results are colorful, flowing, and whimsical. The Marais location has a small section of children's clothes for 2- to 12-year-olds, child versions of the adult styles, toward the back of the store. Additional location: Antik Batik, Collections Femme et Enfant, 26, rue St-Sulpice, 6th arr., **M** St-Sulpice.

Antoine et Lili

95, quai de Valmy, 10th arr.

01.40.37.58.14

M Jacques Bonsergent

www.antoineetlili.com

Monday–Saturday 10am–7pm

Clothes

The three shops that comprise Antoine and Lili—one for children's clothes, one for adult fashion, and one for home décor—occupy an idyllic spot just across from Canal St-Martin. The easy-to-spot, pink, yellow, and green store façades are a well-recognized part of the Parisian cityscape, often seen in the background of French movies and TV shows. The fanciful spirit of this label's designs and fabrics has garnered a loyal following. The bubblegum-pink shop displays clothes, accessories, toys, and costumes for children 6 months to 10 years old. There are strong Asian and Indian influences in the prints and colors, but you'll find classic European looks here, too. Antoine and Lili manages to be comparatively less expensive than other boutiques that carry items made in France.

L'Atelier Si Petit

23, rue des Blancs Manteaux, 4th arr.
01.42.74.09.36
M Rambuteau
www.atelier-sipetit.com
Monday noon–7pm; Tuesday–Saturday 10:30am–7pm; Sunday 2:30–6:30pm
Clothes

Sophie Garreau has designed, fabricated, and sold Si Petit, her brand of children's clothing for 0- to 12-year-olds, since 1989. There are two locations in the Marais, this boutique-workshop and a retail shop on rue de Birague, just steps from the Place des Vosges. Madame Garreau tends the shop herself on many days; she designs and sews on others. Fleece, cotton, linen, and bamboo are her fabrics of choice. Styles are basic, comfortable, and classic. On the mezzanine above the retail store on the ground floor customers can see the workspace where Si Petit's clothing is actually sewn. The chance

to see the creation of a product, especially in a world capital like Paris, makes Si Petit a rare treat.

Additional location: Si Petit, 9, rue de Birague, 4th arr., **M** St-Paul or Bastille.

BHV (Bazar de l'Hôtel de Ville)

52–64, rue de Rivoli, 4th arr.

01.42.74.90.00

M Hôtel de Ville

Daily 9:30am (Monday, Tuesday, Thursday, Friday until 7:30pm; Wednesday until 9pm; Saturday until 8pm); closed Sunday

Clothes, Toys, Baby Gear, Books, Crafts

Many Parisians think of BHV as the city's "affordable" department store. It may have a bigger selection of less expensive brands than those carried by the other *grands magasins*, but in general, its prices are on par with those of more luxurious department stores. Children's clothing, toys, baby gear, and the maternity section are on the 5th floor. In the clothing department, you'll find French labels including IKKS, Petit Bateau, Cadet Rouselle, and Baby Kenzo along with international brands. BHV stocks a fair selection of baby supplies— including umbrella strollers and larger buggies, car seats, Vulli items (Sophie la Giraffe), bottles, bibs, highchairs, carriers—as well as a large Béaba section. The toy department has many French and international brands and characters. There's an excellent selection of the classic French brand Corolle dolls and doll clothes.

Restrooms with a changing station and the store's **cafés** are also on this level making it easy for parents to divide and conquer; one can shop while the other enjoys a snack (and a brilliant view) with the kids.

La Cantine du Bazar full-service cafeteria on the 5th floor is a convenient choice for families. Huge picture windows in the dining area offer spectacular views of Paris's rooftops and the neighboring Hôtel de Ville; it's stocked with high chairs and has lots of room for strollers and playful children. Long, lunchroom-style tables provide comfortable seating for large families. It's not haute cuisine, but the food in BHV's cafeteria is consistently good and popular with locals. The child-friendly environment is virtually unrivaled in Paris; it's a breath of fresh air if you've had to endure, with young ones, a slow-moving meal in a cramped café. The children's menu has a choice of chicken nuggets or *steak haché* (ground beef), drink, and dessert (6,1€). There's also a vegetable and salad buffet and warm plates like roast chicken (6,5€) and various pastas. Daily 11:15am–6pm, Wednesday until 8:30pm; snacks served 9:30am–7:15pm, Wednesday until 8:45pm.

Filament

10, rue Lesdiguières, 4th arr.

01.42.09.81.83

M Bastille

Tuesday–Saturday 11:30am–1:30pm; 2:30pm–7:30pm

Filament Paris, Facebook page

Toys

Filament's vintage-inspired windows lure shoppers with elaborate electric trains traveling a scenic path; next to the choochoo, a group of automated animal marionettes mesmerizes potential customers. Locals look forward to the changing of these intricate *vitrines* as a neighborhood event. Once you've seen the captivating window displays, it's almost impossible to resist walking into this toy-cum-shoe store where the old-fashioned cash register and artisan toys give a nod to yesteryear. The shop is filled with a grand and varied collection of products: dolls, handmade doll clothes, ride-ons, sand toys, model airplanes, puzzles, costumes, and loads of wooden toys. Also sold are shoe brands such as Pom d'Api as well as child-sized espadrilles, imported from Basque country in dozens of colors.

Finger in the Nose

60, rue de Saintonge, 3rd arr.

01.42.71.43.40

M Filles du Calvaire

www.fingerinthenose.com

Tuesday–Saturday 11am–7pm

Clothes

Finger in the Nose describes its style as "a touch of rock and roll attitude with a dose of functionality." Comfortable, long-wearing jeans in a number of washes are the brand's specialty; adult styles have been reworked and adapted for children 3 months to 16 years. The label's color palette is typically dark or muted—black, blue, gray, denim, an occasional red or white—with some plaids. This upper-Marais shop is known for down jackets, wools, knits, and tees imprinted with artistic graphics that children love—animals, super-heroes, motorcycles, and mythological creatures. Sweaters are made with the label's signature thumbhole. Kids like the novelty of sliding their thumbs into the small hole in the sleeve's wrist to stop the sleeve from riding up when putting on another layer.

Gaëlle Barré

17, rue Keller, 11th arr.
01.43.14.63.02
M Bastille
www.gaellebarre.com
Tuesday–Saturday 11:30am–7:30pm
Clothes

Rue Keller is lined with eclectic indie boutiques of all sorts offering music, fashion, comic books, and gadgets. In the midst of it all, the fashion designer Gaëlle Barré, who expanded her fashion repertoire in 2007 to include children's clothes, celebrates the whimsy of youth with sparkly-threaded fabrics, comfortable cuts, and retro-inspired styles in sizes for 3 months to 10 years. Clothes run mid-range in price for a boutique of this size, with girls' dresses around 75€.

Grand Bonton

5, boulevard des Filles du Calvaire, 3rd arr.

01.42.72.34.69

M Filles du Calvaire

www.bonton.fr

Monday–Saturday 10am–7pm

Clothes, Accessories, Décor, Books

Bonton added a playful twist to the elegant, refined look of Bonpoint by bringing vivid color, playground-friendly fabrics, and a lower price point to the parent line's classic styles. Grand Bonton, founded in 2001 by the son and daughter-in-law of Bonpoint's founders, now flourishes as a separate brand with its own distinct look.

There's plenty of eye candy for adults and children in this 8500-square-foot, three-level, modern-meets-old-fashioned-Paris retail

space — Paris's largest children's concept store. In addition to the season's clothing collection for children 0–12 years old, the store stocks a well-edited selection of books, toys, and decorative items. Linens, bedroom furniture, shoes, newborn gifts, and scores of hipster novelties, cleverly displayed with an air of joy and whimsy, tempt shoppers regardless of parental status. The clothes are expensive: a cotton peasant blouse for girls is 63€, a lovely but basic cotton dress 68€, a boys' wool-blend turtleneck sweater 78€, although the mini net bag, like those the French take to the market, is a reasonable 11€ and makes a great souvenir. The displays are delightful and worth a look for style ideas even if you're not prepared to invest in an ensemble.

Grand Bonton has an all-age hair salon as well as a book and movie corner and an irresistible **candy shop-cum-tearoom**. Hot chocolate, tea, coffee, *viennoiseries*, cookies, brownies, fruit juices, and candy, of course, are on the menu. Everyone seems to enjoy the 1970s photo booth that spits out a strip of black-and-white photos; at 2€, it's a cheap thrill and an enduring souvenir.

Additional locations: Bonton, 82, rue de Grenelle, 7th arr., **M** Rue du Bac; Bonton Bazar, 122, rue du Bac, 7th arr., **M** Sèvres-Babylone; Bébé Bonton, 82, rue de Grenelle, 7th arr., **M** Rue du Bac; Papillon Bonton, 82, rue de Grenelle, 7th arr., **M** Rue du Bac.

I Love My Blender
36, rue du Temple, 4th arr.
01.42.77.50.32
M Rambuteau
www.ilovemyblender.fr
Tuesday–Saturday 10am–7pm; Sunday 10am–6pm
Books

From its front window with bright colors and dangling trinkets, this quirky little bookshop looks like it could be a toy store. Inside it's stocked with an impeccable and vast selection of books by anglophone authors from all over the world. According to shop owner Christophe Persouyre, the haphazard organization of the books is intentional. It encourages customers to come to him, share their tastes, and seek advice and recommendations. He is passionate about this interaction and it is this personal contact that his loyal clientele finds so endearing. Young readers can peruse a thoughtful selection of children's titles at a child-sized table. I Love My Blender also has a limited array of gifts that include children's toys, candles, stationery, and tea.

ie
128, rue Vieille du Temple, 3rd arr.
01.44.59.87.72
M Filles du Calvaire
www.ieboutique.com
Tuesday–Sunday 11am–8pm
Clothes, Décor, Fabric

Behind the ie brand, which means "house" in Japanese, are a Franco-Nepali architect/lighting designer and a Japanese stylist/textile designer. Together they create children's clothing, linens, and decorative household items. Ie's clothing line is made in India from colorful handwoven and printed natural fabrics. The result is comfortable, relatively inexpensive boutique clothing that loosely follows the lines of classic French styles.

Lilli Bulle

3, rue de la Forge Royale, 11th arr.
01.43.73.71.63
M Ledru-Rollin
www.lillibulle.com
Tuesday–Friday 10am–1:30pm, 3–7pm; Saturday 11am–7pm
Clothes, Accessories, Toys, Décor

Lilli Bulle features products from more than 100 designers and creative brands under one roof in its boutique. The number of items is overwhelming. Toys, games, and stuffed animals are displayed at a child's height while clothing and accessories are at parent-height; this may prove dangerous depending on your little ones. The space is also used for art exhibitions and story times, some of which are in English. Lilli Bulle connects clients with local artists who can be commissioned for custom murals and other creative work.

Little French Trotters

28, rue de Charonne, 11th arr.
01.43.57.04.09
M Ledru-Rollin
www.frenchtrotters.fr
Tuesday–Saturday 11:30am–7:30pm
Clothes, Shoes

Parisian parents in search of an alternative to the Bonpoint look, who desire an edgier style in clothes and shoes for kids 3 months to

10 years old, head to Little French Trotters. This multi-brand boutique captures the indie spirit with its selection of labels like Zef, Troizenfants, Bobo Choses, and Finger in the Nose. The shop also has a small selection of books and toys.

La Maison du Cerf Volant

7, rue de Prague, 12th arr.
01.44.68.00.75
M Ledru-Rollin
www.lamaisonducerfvolant.com
Tuesday–Saturday 11am–7pm
Kites

Across the street from bookstore La Terrasse de Gutenberg is this fanciful kite boutique that features every imaginable *cerf volant* from simple to complex, inexpensive to indulgent. It sells equipment for kiteboarding like the kite buggy, a lightweight vehicle powered by a giant traction kite, as well as mountain boards and an elaborate selection of boomerangs.

Le Marchand d'Étoiles

65, rue de Turenne, 3rd arr.
01.42.71.68.12
M Chemin Vert
www.marchand-etoiles.com
Tuesday–Saturday 10:30am–7pm
Clothes

Le Marchand d'Étoiles's namesake brand of ultra-comfortable pajamas for children 0–12 years old, are decidedly cute and fashionable enough to wear all day. Parents appreciate the value of this pajama-to-play concept; the brand is now carried in dozens of boutiques in Paris, around France, and in a handful of shops internationally. The line features soft fabrics and simple styles of sleepwear, infant bodysuits, and underwear, a few accessories such as scarves, and fabric mobiles.

Mes Premiers Pas

32, rue St-Paul, 4th arr.

M St-Paul

01.42.78.26.74

Mes Premiers Pas, créateurs, Facebook page

Tuesday 10:30am–4pm; Wednesday–Saturday 10:30am–7pm; Sunday 3–7pm

Clothing

This charming little shop with gentle, muted light and exposed stonework gathers together independent labels for children 0 to 8 years old with an emphasis on up-and-coming French designers like Je suis en CP! and les Petits Parisiens, organic brands Aravore and La Queue du Chat, and the Spanish brand Pequeño Tocon. The boutique also features accessories, furniture, bags, totes, backpacks, and original work from local artists.

Monoprix

71, rue St-Antoine, 4th arr.

01.42.74.13.73

M St-Paul

www.monoprix.fr

Monday–Saturday 9am–10pm

Clothes, Baby Care, Snacks

This convenient and well-stocked Monoprix carries every possible necessity and then some: infant and children's clothing, diapers, baby care basics, and groceries.

Mum & Babe

3, rue Keller 11th arr.
01.43.38.83.55
M Ledru-Rollin, Bastille
www.mumandbabe.fr
Tuesday – Saturday 9:30am – 6:30pm
Salon

Mum & Babe is a full-service day spa and salon that includes baby-sitting for 0- to 6-year-olds — every city should have one of these. The salon's palette of rose, lavender, and gray soothes mothers who stop in for a moment of pampering. Children play in a cozy central area with games, toys and large windows that make it easy for parents to peek in for an unobtrusive check. The staff is kind and attentive; language isn't a problem for babies or young children with French sitters. The day spa also offers workshops for infant massage, baby signing, and how to use an infant-wrap carrier. Reservations are required.

Niou

11, rue St-Paul, 4th arr.
01.48.87.24.21
M St-Paul
www.niou.fr
Tuesday – Saturday 11am – 1pm, 2:30 – 7pm; Sunday 2:30 – 6:30pm; closed Monday
Toys

A neighborhood favorite, Niou is piled floor to ceiling with a carefully selected inventory of not-so-commercial toys and products for 0- to 12-year-olds. You'll find modern and traditional toys as well as costumes, games, music boxes, and hand puppets in this stroller-friendly shop. A handsome selection of reusable water bottles and baby carriers is a welcome find for traveling families. Niou also has a number of extraordinary costumes and pajamas including pirate and chevalier PJs (28€) and an "ermine"-trimmed, red velvet King's cape and crown (42€, 29,9€).

L'Ourson en Bois

83, rue Charenton, 12th arr.
01.40.01.02.40
M Ledru-Rollin
Monday–Saturday 10am–7pm
Toys

L'Ourson en Bois's crimson façade with gold lettering and delicately styled window displays evokes the toy stores of yesteryear. Inside it's a treasure chest: infant toys from Lilliputiens, stuffed animals by

Moulin Roty, puzzles, Papo figurines, costumes, and mobiles. Although the focus is on European brands, a handful of more commercial names like Hello Kitty are also represented. One of the most fun things about this shop is the collection of dozens of small containers filled with little toys like whistles and springs, all for 1€.

Petit Bateau

36, rue de Sévigné, 3rd arr.
01.48.87.27.10
M St-Paul
www.petit-bateau.fr
Monday–Saturday 10am–7pm
Clothes

A French standard in children's clothing, Petit Bateau is best known for its soft cotton fabrics and the *marinière*, the traditional sailor's shirt with dark blue and white horizontal stripes. Many Petit Bateau products are still produced in the company's original factory. In addition to the 10 boutiques in Paris, the brand is sold in several department and concept stores in the city and through an online store. Petit Bateau creates clothing for newborns, children up to 12 years old, men, and women.

Petit Pan

39 and 76, rue François Miron, 4th arr.
01.44.54.90.84
M St-Paul
www.petitpan.com
Monday–Saturday 10:30am–2pm, 3–7:30pm
Clothing, Décor

The couple who owns Petit Pan—a Chinese kite designer and a Belgian artist—have created a label that reinterprets classic Asian prints and styles informed by a modern Parisian aesthetic. The concept was inspired by a newborn's ensemble, handmade by Pan Gang's mother in China, for the birth of the couple's first son. Artist Myriam de Loor recalls her immediate reaction, "I loved the richness of the print: small, sparkling, bold patterns and bright colors, just the way I like them. I was amazed by this comfortable and cozy outfit worn by children in faraway lands."

The shop at #76 is an airy and magical space strung with fanciful garlands, with kites and mobiles hanging from the ceiling. The shelves are filled with bath towels, school bags, smocks, chair cushions, toiletry pouches, and other household accessories all made in Petit Pan's signature prints (5€–22€). You'll have to look up to see some of Pan's most stunning items—dangling mobiles made from bamboo and hand-painted silk, adorned with 3-dimensional shapes and figures. The selection changes frequently; themes often reference sea creatures, insects, and space exploration (35€–98€).

The Petit Pan boutique across the street at #39 sells the brand's fabrics by the meter, both plain and wax-coated, the latter perfect for sewing raincoats or outdoor tablecloths (18€–21€). It's as tempting

as a candy store inside; dozens of jars line the shelves, brimming with brightly colored treasures—fabric-covered buttons, sequins, metallic beads, miniature animal-shaped bells, pompoms, and countless other captivating embellishments.

Les Petits Bla-blas
7, rue de Crussol, 11th arr.
06.15.91.68.47
M Filles du Calvaire, Oberkampf
www.lespetitsblablas.com
Tuesday–Saturday noon–7pm
Clothes, Décor

Yet another Parisian concept store that assembles the coolest of the cool with a dollop of retro flair: Japanese dolls, vintage-styled kids' T-shirts, fabric, games, decorative items, bed linens, toys, and clothing for kids 0 to 8 years old. The nondescript, gray storefront belies the quirky and colorful world owner Pascaline Delcourt has created behind it. She says she creates simple styles that are "retro, funny, joyful, chic, original." Inspired by Japanese and American fabrics, Delcourt creates her own line of clothing and accessories, manufactured in France, to which the shop owes its name.

Pop Market

50, rue Bichat, 10th arr.
09.52.79.96.86
M Jacques Bonsergent
www.popmarket.fr
Tuesday–Friday 11am–3pm, 4–7:30pm; Saturday 11am–7:30pm; Sunday 3–7pm
Toys

Head to Pop Market for a colorful and diverse mix of fashion accessories, books, paper products, and decorative objects. There's a section devoted entirely to children with an ever-changing but always playful choice of lunch boxes, pencil pouches, toys, gadgets, games, stickers, art supplies, and more. Pop Market is a great boutique for unique low- to mid-priced souvenirs.

The Red Wheelbarrow Bookstore

22, rue St-Paul, 4th arr.
01.48.04.75.08
M St-Paul
The Red Wheelbarrow Bookshop Paris, Facebook page
Monday 10am–6pm; Tuesday–Saturday 10am–7pm; Sunday 2–6pm
Books

Books are stacked clear to the ceiling on rustic 2-by-4s in this independent English-language bookstore. There's a smattering of kids' books in the front of the shop. In the back you'll find a generous children's section that trails around a corner. The shop's staff is welcoming, full of recommendations for locals and tourists alike.

La Terrasse de Gutenberg
9, rue Emilio Castelar, 12th arr.
01.43.07.42.15
M Ledru-Rollin
Tuesday–Sunday 10am–8pm
Books

Near Marché Aligré is the kind of neighborhood bookshop one dreams about: loads of books (in French) tended to by an enthusiastic, well-read, and approachable staff. Kids will enjoy the roomy yet cozy reading area created especially for them. It's a space that takes the fear out of a foreign language, inviting children to open and investigate French children's books. It doesn't merit a special trip, but if you're in the area and want to pick up a book for your little ones, it's a worthwhile stop.

Thanksgiving
20, rue St-Paul, 4th arr.
01.42.77.68.29
M St-Paul
www.thanksgivingparis.com
Tuesday–Saturday 10:30am–7pm; Sunday 11am–6pm
Food

Thanksgiving sells many of the American (processed) grocery items you — but probably not your children — hope you've left far behind across the Atlantic: Pop Tarts, Kraft Macaroni and Cheese, and Cheerios. It does, however, stock virtually impossible-to-find products that could come in handy if you've rented an apartment: pancake syrup, U.S.-style bacon, baking powder and soda, pancake mixes, refried beans, Hellman's mayonnaise, and yellow mustard, not to mention all of the fixings for a Thanksgiving feast.

Troizenfants

14, rue de Turenne, 4th arr.
01.42.74.44.95
M St-Paul
Tuesday–Saturday 11am–2pm, 3–7pm; Sunday 2–7pm
www.troizenfants.com
Clothes

Troizenfants was founded when two mothers, one a stylist, the other a model, partnered to create a line of children's clothing that was fashionable and affordable. The boutique displays impeccably styled designs for kids 3 months to 12 years old, more playful and practical than some of the other big French children's brands. For a French boutique label with a style and quality on par with Bonpoint, it's relatively less expensive: the *foulard elastiqué*—a scarf worn by young French girls to keep their hair back (12,5€), bucket and baseball hats (22,5€), a boys' wool turtleneck sweater (65€), a cotton dress in a miniature-flower print (58€), and an undeniably adorable velour winter coat for baby (78€).

Additional locations: 22, rue Houdon, 18th arr., **M** Abbesses; Troizenfants Galeries Lafayette, 40, boulevard Haussman, 5th floor, 9th arr., **M** Chaussée d'Antin-La Fayette.

STAY

Apartment rental is the best option for families who want to stay in the Marais district. I've found that many Marais hotels cater to adult couples; for those that do welcome travelers with young children, amenities like baby beds are a scarcity and rooms seem particularly small, even for Paris. Look for an apartment in the neighborhoods around Métro stations St-Paul, Hôtel de Ville, and Pont Marie as they are especially central to Paris's most popular attractions.

PLAY

EAT

SHOP

STAY

PLAY

Batobus

08.25.05.01.01

www.batobus.com

April 6–September 2, departures every 20 minutes from 10am–9:30pm; September 3–April 5, departures every 25 minutes from 10am–7pm.

1-day pass for adults 15€; 15 and under 7€; 3 and under free (2 and 5 consecutive day passes also available).

Departs from eight locations: Notre Dame Cathedral-Quai de Montebello-5th arr., St-Germain-des-Prés-Quai Malaquais-6th arr., Jardin des Plantes-Quai St-Bernard-5th arr., Champs-Élysées-near Pont Alexandre III-8th arr., Louvre-Quai du Louvre-1st arr., Hôtel de Ville-Quai de l'Hôtel de Ville-4th arr., Tour Eiffel-Port de la Bourdonnais-7th arr., Musée d'Orsay-Quai de Solférino-7th arr.

Hop-on-and-off boat tours are convenient for short stays in Paris. They're a good way to see the city's major sights quickly and with minimal frustration. The boat tours are a bit more challenging than similar bus tours for those traveling with young children because of the steep walk down many stairs to reach the Seine-side boarding points.

Bike About Tours

Meet at Charlemagne statue in front of Notre Dame Cathedral, 4th arr.

06.18.80.84.92

M Cité, Hôtel de Ville

www.bikeabouttours.com

May 15–October 2 daily at 10am and 3pm; October 3–December 1 daily at 10am; February 15–April 5 daily at 10am; April 6–May 14 Monday–Friday at 10am, Saturday–Sunday at 10am and 3pm

The group tour is best with children 10 years and older. Private family bike tours are also available. Participants meet next to the Charlemagne statue on the plaza in front of Notre Dame Cathedral before walking to the nearby Vinci parking garage on rue de Lobau to pick up bikes.

Cathédrale Notre-Dame de Paris

Place du Parvis-de-Notre-Dame, 4th arr.

01.42.34.56.10

M Cité

www.notredamedeparis.fr

Daily 8am–6:45pm, Sunday until 7:15pm. Free 90-minute tours in English Wednesday and Thursday at 2pm, and Saturday at 2:30pm. Public toilets are located next to the statue of Charlemagne; his horse's tail points to a blue and white sign that marks the stairway down to the restrooms.

France's most famous cathedral, Notre Dame, offers jaw-dropping views from every vantage. Be sure to circle the entire structure on foot. Stand in the main plaza in front of the church, the Parvis, and help your children find Point Zéro, a small octagonal brass plate engraved with a compass star that reads Point Zéro des Routes de France. In 1924, it was decided that this spot would mark the point from which all distances from Paris to the rest of France are measured. It's located approximately 100 feet in front of Notre Dame's main entrance.

From Point Zéro, gaze a dizzying 400 feet upwards to the top of the bell towers. Walk Seine-side for a better view of the spectacular flying buttresses. Parents with younger children can alternate longer visits to the cathedral with stints at the Square Jean XXIII playground, located immediately behind Notre Dame. Kids 3 to 7 years old can swing, spin, rock, dig, and climb at this well-located play area. Benches are everywhere in the square; it makes a beautiful spot to enjoy a picnic lunch or a crêpe from one of the nearby vendors.

Before visiting, check the *Children's* site, under the *Cathedral for Art and History* tab, on the cathedral's main website in English. Written for children, this section answers basic but useful questions like "What is a cathedral?" It also includes information on Notre Dame's history, architecture, stained-glass windows, organ, bells, and famous gargoyles.

Even young children will be struck by the soaring ceilings, colorful windows, and the enormity of Notre-Dame de Paris's interior. Built between 1163 and 1272, with countless intermittent renovations, this was the site for the coronations, baptisms, and marriages of French royalty and rulers.

Tours de la Cathédrale Notre-Dame de Paris

Rue du Cloître Notre-Dame, 4th arr.

01.53.40.60.80

notre-dame-de-paris.monuments-nationaux.fr/en/

Daily, weather permitting, from April 1–September 30, 10am–
6:30pm; Saturday and Sunday 10am–11pm in June, July, August;
October 1–March 31, 10am–5:30pm; last visit 45 minutes before
closing; closed January 1, May 1, December 25.

Adults 8€; 18–25 5€; free for under 18. No toilet facilities or
elevator.

Best for children 7 years and older

Lines form on the north side of the church (the left side as you face
the front entrance to the cathedral). Climb more than 400 stairs to
enjoy the sublime panoramic view of Paris and to get a closer look
at Quasimodo's domain. It's 300 steps to the The Grand Gallery (La
Grande Galerie or La Galerie des Chimères), where your eyes meet
those of the famous yet disturbing gargoyles and grotesques. It's
just a few more steps up the south tower to visit the colossal 13-ton
bell, le Bourdon, which rings on important holidays and events.

Kids inevitably want to know more about the scary sculptures.
Gargoyles function as part of a building's drainage system; they help
to deliver water away from its sides to minimize erosive damage.
Chimères or grotesques, like those that adorn La Galérie des
Chimères (Grand Gallery) that connects the north and south towers,
are purely decorative and non-functioning; they were added during
Viollet-le-Duc's 19th-century restoration of the cathedral. The spire
was also added during this restoration; the rooster who sits at the
very top is said to contain three religious relics: a fragment of the

Crown of Thorns and relics from France's patron saint, St-Denis, and Paris's patron saint, Ste-Geneviève.

In high tourist season, arrive very early since lines can be unbearably long; expect a wait of approximately two hours. The climb is more appropriate for children older than 7, but it depends on your little ones' stamina—or yours, if you're carrying them. Check the website for any exceptional closings. A useful printout about the history and architectural evolution of Notre Dame and its towers is available in English on the Towers' official website under the *Visit* tab, then *Documents* menu.

La Conciergerie

2, boulevard du Palais, 1st arr.

01.53.40.60.80

M Cité

conciergerie.monuments-nationaux.fr

Daily March–October, 9:30am–6pm; November–February, 9am–5pm

Adults 7€; free for under 18

Best for 7 years and older

This former part of a royal palace turned notorious prison in the 14th century held almost 3,000 of those sentenced to death during the French Revolution. Its more famous prisoners include Ravaillac, the extremist monk who murdered King Henri IV, and, later, Marie-Antoinette and Robespierre. Highlights include prison cells, the Guardroom, and the Hall of Men-at-Arms, an enormous room that functioned as a dining room for a staff that numbered approximately 2,000.

Visitors can see where poor prisoners were housed as well as living quarters for those who could afford to pay for better-appointed chambers, including a recreation of Marie-Antoinette's cell (a chapel now occupies what was her room). Wax figures help illustrate a prisoner's living conditions in this antechamber to the guillotine; the visit also describes what typically transpired on their day of execution—as the condemned were led to death, their hair and shirt collar were cut to facilitate the task at hand.

The Conciergerie's four towers border the Seine. France's first public clock was installed in the rectangular tower, la Tour de l'Horloge, in 1370. The round tower farthest from the clock tower is known as la Tour Bonbec. It owes its name to la Salle de Question, the torture chamber or interrogation room, that was located inside. *Bon bec* is a French expression once used to describe a person who talks a lot; even the most reluctant of prisoners could be persuaded to confess inside Bonbec.

Le Marché aux Fleurs et aux Oiseaux Cité
Place Louis Lépine and quai de la Corse, 4th arr.
M Cité
Flower Market daily 8am–7:30pm; Bird Market Sunday 8am–7:30pm
This manageably sized outdoor market is an entertaining diversion for children. Thousands of flowers, shrubs, and trees are on display or for sale. Sundays, the market is an animated venue for the sale of birds and small animals.

Mémorial des Martyrs de la Déportation

Square de l'Île de France, 7, quai de l'Archêveché, 4th arr.

01.46.33.87.56

M Cité; RER: St-Michel-Notre-Dame

Monday–Saturday 10am–noon, 2–7pm in summer; until 5pm in winter

Located at the very tip of Île St-Louis, behind Notre Dame cathedral, this is a somber and moving memorial to 200,000 people who were deported to Nazi concentration camps during World War II. Of those, approximately 76,000 were Jewish and 11,000 of that number were children. Descending the stairs to the entrance of the memorial there is a sense of a separation from the city above. Visitors enter a narrow, intentionally confining hall that leads past 200,000 back-lit crystals sparkling in tribute to each victim; an eternal flame of hope burns at the end of the passage.

La Sainte-Chapelle

4, boulevard du Palais, 1st arr.

01.53.40.60.80

M Cité, St-Michel

sainte-chapelle.monuments-nationaux.fr/en

March 1 to October 31, 9:30am–6pm; November 1–February 28, 9am–5pm; Wednesdays May 15–September 15; last admission at 9pm

Adults 7,5€; free for under 18 if accompanied by an adult. Combined discounted ticket with Conciergerie: adults 11€; free for under 18. Visits in English or French daily at 11am, 3pm, and 4pm; contact the monument directly at the number listed to learn of any last-minute changes in English tour availability.

Try to visit this spectacular chapel on a day when the sun is shining. The 50-foot stained-glass windows cast a glow that will fascinate children as well as adults. The jewels of the chapel, its stained-glass windows, were used to recount stories from the Bible. The windows should be read beginning from left to right, from bottom to top.

The Sainte-Chapelle was built to house important relics purchased by King Louis IX from Emperor Baldwin II of Constantinople in 1239; most notable among these was what is traditionally considered to be the Crown of Thorns worn by Jesus (the Crown is now held in Notre Dame Cathedral). The chapel's richly painted interior is also worth pointing out to children. Remind them that while the inside of many ancient churches now appear gray or austere, most of them were once similarly painted.

Parcours Découverte, a colorful brochure for kids with educational information and games written in French, is available to download from the French website (under *Publics*, select the *Jeune Public* tab).

Vedettes du Pont Neuf

Square du Vert Galant, 1st arr.

01.46.33.98.38

M Pont Neuf

www.vedettesdupontneuf.com

March 15–October 31 daily every 45 minutes 10:30am–12pm; closed 12–1:30pm; every ½ hour 1:30–7pm, 9–10:30pm; on the hour from 7–9pm; November 1–March 14 daily every 45 minutes 10:30am–6:30pm; closed 12–2pm; one cruise at 8pm and 10pm; Friday–Sunday there is an additional cruise at 9pm.

Adults 13€; 4–12 years 7€; 3 and under free. Purchasing and printing a ticket online will save each paying passenger 4€–5€.

These one-hour Seine river sightseeing cruises with commentary in English and French from a tour guide (rather than a recording), depart near Pont Neuf. It's a steep walk down the stairs to the quay; those with strollers will have to collapse them to descend. Boat cruises offer an expedient overview of Paris's top sights; it's a beautiful, child-friendly vantage from which to enjoy the monuments.

EAT

Berthillon

31, rue St-Louis en l'Île, 4th arr.

01.43.54.31.61

M Pont Marie

www.berthillon.fr

Wednesday–Sunday 10am–8pm; closed Monday and Tuesday; closed for approximately six weeks in summer (end of July–beginning of September)

Berthillon has been the gold standard for Parisian ice cream since it was founded over 50 years ago. The more than 30 flavors of sorbet and ice cream vary seasonally, are made on site, and are preservative-free. Among the flavors are a sublime salted-butter caramel, wild strawberry, mandarine chocolate, peach, red grapefruit, rhubarb, Earl Grey tea, gingerbread, caramel pear, and of course vanilla and chocolate (2,3€ single, 3,6€ double take-away).

When lines are long at the take-away window, look for a spot in the adjacent tearoom. The children's dish includes a choice of two flavors in a cone or cup (4,7€). Also on the menu is a simple sundae served with a choice of ice cream, syrup, and whipped cream (5,5€). The tearoom, with its paneled walls and dark green marble tables, evokes a feeling of old Paris. A dessert case in the center of the room tempts customers with tarte tatin, macarons, and other pastries. Breakfast, fresh-pressed juices, coffee, and teas are also served. The tables are small, but a comfortable and toddler-friendly banquette runs along the walls. Berthillon's ice creams and sorbets are offered in many Parisian cafés and restaurants, so even during the shop's summer closing, you can find a taste. Or, if the lines are impossibly long and you need an alternative, Amorino gelato at #47, rue St-Louis en l'Île, and My Berry frozen yogurt at #51, are both just a few blocks up the street.

Boulangerie Martin
40, rue St-Louis en l'Île, 4th arr.
01.43.54.69.48
M Pont Marie
Tuesday–Saturday 7:30am–2pm, 3–8pm
This lovely vintage bakery opened in the 1930s and has been in the care of the Martin family since 1968. It's known for its organic wheat baguette and exquisitely buttery croissants. The changing selection of other *viennoiseries* and pastries are worth a taste: caramel cake, meringues, brioche, and almond croissants.

Calixte
64, rue St-Louis en l'Île, 4th arr.
01.43.26.42.28
M Pont Marie
Daily 8am–2pm, 4–8pm
Parisians crowd this gourmet shop for snacks before heading to meet their children at Île St-Louis's public *école maternelle* (preschool) just a few blocks down at #21. Calixte sells a bit of every-thing from croissants to candies to sweeter pastries such as strawberry, fig, or lemon tartes, and the dazzling Clementine Chocolat. The savory selection of miniature quiches and *terrines en croûte* pack well for a Seine-side picnic.

La Charlotte de l'Îsle

24, rue St-Louis en l'Île, 4th arr.
01.43.54.25.83
M Pont Marie
www.lacharlottedelisle.fr
Wednesday–Sunday 11am–7pm

This salon de thé sits smack dab in the middle of the Île-St-Louis and revels in its old-fashioned ways. After more than 30 years of making irresistible desserts from scratch, owner Sylvie Langlet handed over the reins to La Charlotte's new owner, Madame Asma Soula, in 2011. Soula, who spent 10 years working in Japan, vowed to continue the shop's tradition of creating homemade desserts from natural ingredients without preservatives.

Soula's own favorites include classic cakes, dense sweet loaves in variations such as orange blossom (*fleurs d'oranger*), a chocolate and Madagascar vanilla marble cake, and a citrus-infused *cake au citron*. La Charlotte serves a variety of teas and artisan hot chocolate (7€). Every other Wednesday afternoon the tearoom hosts an activity for children (in French): musical story time, marionette performances, or workshops like Japanese floral arrangement and origami. Check the website for reservations and more information.

Le Flore en l'Île

42, quai d'Orléans, 4th arr.
01.43.29.88.27
M Pont Marie
Daily 10:30am–9:30pm; Sunday 10:30am–3:30pm

The roomy terrace at this corner café, popular with tourists and Parisians alike, has stunning views of the Seine and the towers of

Notre Dame. The café's interior is tiny, but there's room for strollers towards the front of the patio. With its pastries, sweet crêpes, and 10 delicious flavors of ice cream to eat in or take away, Le Flore en l'Île is best at teatime or for a snack. The menu, translated into English, has a few mains that might appeal to kids: scrambled eggs and bacon (9,5€), a club sandwich (15€), and roast chicken (17€).

Le Lutétia

33, quai Bourbon, 4th arr.
01.40.51.80.30
M Pont Marie
Daily 11:30am–11pm with continuous service

The bustling Le Lutétia brasserie, on a corner of Île-St-Louis that seems less touristy than others, has superb views of the Seine. Le Lutétia offers friendly service, a generous terrace, consistently tasty food, and a posted menu without an English translation — something rarely seen in this part of Paris. At the height of the lunch hour it's packed with locals, understandable with its affordable 14,6€ menu. The bacon cheeseburger with french fries (14€), fresh salads (13,5€–15€), lasagna, and hamburgers, available à la carte, or more traditional items such as steak tartare, grilled fish, or steak frites might pique the interest of your family.

SHOP

L'Arche de Noë

70, rue St-Louis en l'Île, 4th arr.
01.46.34.61.60
M Pont Marie
Daily 10:30am–1:30pm, 2–7pm
Toys

This charming toyshop ("Noah's Ark") specializes in wooden toys and stuffed animals. It has an impressive range of toys: crafts, stickers, crafting clay, card games, music boxes, Moulin Roty lovies (*doudous*), doctor kits, water bottles, tableware, costumes, even a Bingo set that teaches the most important monuments in Paris. The store sells European characters like Barbapapa and a small selection of international brands like Barbie and Littlest Pet Shop. In spite of its expensive location, prices are competitive with other toy stores in central Paris. The staff is friendly and helpful, but pay attention to their bold posted sign and finish up any ice cream before entering.

Clair de Rêve

35, rue St-Louis en l'Île, 4th arr.
01.43.81.11.37
M Pont Marie
www.clairdereve.com
Monday–Saturday 11am–1pm, 2:45–7pm
Puppets, Toys

A little bit creepy, a little bit cool, this tiny shop's specialty is artisan-made marionettes. Fantastical puppets dangle from the ceiling;

some appear friendly while others stare with an uncomfortably life-like gaze. The craftsmanship is something to behold; depending on your child, however, the shop's front window may afford the best view (50€–900€+). The boutique also sells music boxes, robots, watches, and wind-up toys. Puppets may be made-to-order in Clair de Rêve's nearby workshop.

Citadines Prestige St-Germain

53 *ter*, quai des Grands Augustins, 6th arr.

01.44.07.70.00

M Pont Neuf, St-Michel

www.citadines.com

Elevator/AC/Wifi

Suites from 300€

Looking out onto the Seine, just across from Île de la Cité via the Pont Neuf, is an ideally located branch of the Citadines chain of Apart'hotels. Most rooms are configured as suites with a foldout sofa in the living room, a separate bedroom, and kitchenette; self-service laundry facilities are also available on site. Daily housekeeping and breakfast is included with some rooms. The accommodations aren't luxurious, but for Paris they are spacious (270–410 square feet) and consistently clean. An extra bed or baby cot is available upon request.

During oppressively hot summers the air-conditioning, virtually non-existent in private apartments, is invaluable with children. Private apartments may be the ideal accommodation, but with a supermarket around the corner and Notre Dame and Paris's most family-friendly neighborhoods just minutes away, this Citadines is an outstanding second choice especially for those staying less than a week.

Hospitel Hôtel Dieu
1, place du Parvis Notre Dame, 4th arr.
01.44.32.01.00
M Cité
www.hotel-hospitel.com
Elevator/AC/Wifi
Doubles from 72€, 11€ extra bed

What a view, what a location—this unexpected hotel is situated on one side of Notre Dame's main plaza on the sixth floor of what is considered Paris's oldest hospital, the Hôtel-Dieu de Paris. It's an unassuming hotel with 14 spotless rooms, as institutional and spartan as you might expect in the middle of a functioning hospital.

The location and price in France's capital, however, are unrivaled. Heading up the stairs past the splendid courtyard garden towards the elevator, notice the historic images that detail the origins of the hospital in 651 c.e. You are sleeping in a building that has been inextricably tied to the fate of this city since its inception. The staff is exceptionally accommodating, which somewhat compensates for its minimal charm. If you're open to a unique experience in a historically significant building — and find comfort in having medical attention just a few feet away — the Hospitel Hôtel Dieu is an excellent choice.

There are no connecting rooms so the hotel works best for a family with an infant or toddler, or with older children who can stay in a separate but adjacent room. There are no cribs or baby cots, but guests are welcome to bring their own or to co-sleep. Extra twin beds are available in some rooms (11€). Accommodations located on the Notre Dame side have views of the towers. In-room breakfast is served from 7am–10am (from 4,5€), and meals from the hospital cafeteria can be delivered to guest rooms (from 10€).

Hôtel du Jeu de Paume
54, rue St-Louis en l'Île, 4th arr.
01.43.26.14.18
M Pont Marie; RER: St-Michel-Notre-Dame
www.jeudepaumehotel.com
Elevator/AC/Wifi
Doubles from 285€; suites and apartments from 450€
This breathtaking boutique hotel was built on the former grounds of a royal Jeu de Paume court; its original structure dates to the early 17th century. By the mid-18th century the game, a precursor of

tennis, had lost its popular appeal and virtually all of the courts were destroyed. In fact, in a metro area that once boasted more than 250 courts, today only two playable ones remain, one in Paris and one at château Fontainebleau.

The wood beams that support the court's ceiling were transformed into a striking centerpiece around which 30 modern guest rooms are now situated. Looking up past five levels of rooms, the building's impressive framework is visible. Guests pass through an immense carriage door from the street, cross a courtyard, then enter the hotel's expansive reception area. Most average-sized rooms can accommodate a baby bed, available upon request. For families with older children there is a two-level, three-person suite (from 450€) as well as first- and second-floor apartments (from 900€ and 620€ respectively). The staircases in the suites may raise some safety concerns as they are not entirely secured by railings. The continental breakfast is pricey at 18€, but there are a number of neighborhood bakeries and cafés in proximity for those who wish to venture out.

Hôtel St-Louis

75, rue St-Louis en l'Île, 4th arr.
01.46.34.04.80
www.saintlouisenlisle.com
M Pont Marie
Elevator/AC/Wifi
Doubles from 189€; triples from 279€

An attentive staff greets guests at this recently renovated five-floor, 20-room hotel in the middle of Île-St-Louis. Even with its modern amenities, the hotel has retained an Old World character with its exposed wooden beams and whitewashed stonework. Rooms are decorated in a soothing neutral color palette and kept impeccably clean. Superior doubles can accommodate a baby bed that is available upon request (from 189€). Triple rooms have a double bed and foldout sofa and while potentially tight, can also be fitted with a baby cot (from 279€). Two rooms on the ground floor are connected by a private hallway and can be booked for larger families or for those with older children; one of the two rooms, equipped for guests with physical challenges, provides extra space and a generously sized shower. A neighboring apartment is also available that can accommodate families with three children (280€/night).

PLAY

EAT

SHOP

STAY

Quartier Latin

PLAY

Arènes de Lutèce

Entrances: 47, rue Monge; 12, rue de Navarre; 4, rue des Arènes, 5th arr.

M Jussieu, Place Monge, Cardinal Lemoine

en.parisinfo.com

Monday–Friday 8am–sunset; Saturday–Sunday 9am–sunset

Free

Minutes away from Jardin des Plantes is a remnant of Paris's ancient past, a Roman arena that has been transformed into a public park. First-century Parisians used the space as a theatre and for circus and sporting events. Historians believe that three of the five niches that open directly into the arena, located beneath the lower bleachers, were used as animal cages. Locals love to picnic on the stone bleachers or on the grass in this space that once accommodated as many as 17,000 spectators. There are free public **restrooms** on the upper terrace of the arena's north side.

La Maison des Oiseaux

Inside Arènes de Lutèce

6, rue des Arènes

01.43.28.47.63

Saturday 1:30–5pm; until 5:30pm, March–October

Free

Located in the square, the Maison des Oiseaux was created to familiarize Parisians with the local bird population; visitors can see more than 100 species that live in the capital.

ARÈNES DE LUTÈCE

Square Capitan
Inside Arènes de Lutèce
6, rue des Arènes, 5th arr.
en.parisinfo.com
Monday–Friday 8am–sunset; Saturday–Sunday 9am–sunset;
hours vary seasonally

A large playground for children 2 to 14 years old is located on the
north side of the arena. It sits shaded by the surrounding apartment buildings, as if it's been carved right out of the middle of
the city. Kids can climb, slide, dig, and rock and ride on one of
the many play structures.

Robert van der Hilst/Gamma-Rapho via Getty Images

Jardin des Plantes

Entrances on rue Cuvier, rue Buffon, rue Geoffroy-St-Hillaire, 5th arr.
M Jussieu (an escalator is available to exit the station; there is a pay
public **toilet** just above ground), Censier-Daubenton
www.mnhn.fr

The Jardin des Plantes, or Botanical Garden, is not the most interesting draw here for young children, but rather the Ménagerie
and the Grande Galérie de l'Evolution located within the garden
grounds—kids will love them both. Aspiring paleontologists will
enjoy the dinosaur exhibits in Les Galeries de Paléontologie et
d'Anatomie Comparée, another museum located within the Jardin
des Plantes. Worth checking out on the rue Buffon side of the garden,

near the paleontology museum, is the Manège à Dodo, a charming carousel populated with extinct and endangered species such as the Tasmanian wolf, Dodo bird, triceratops and horned turtle.

Ménagerie du Jardin des Plantes

Inside Jardin des Plantes
Entrances off of rue Cuvier and through the gardens
01.40.79.37.94
M Jussieu
www.mnhn.fr
Daily 9am–5pm; April–September until 6pm
Adults 9€; 4–16 years 7€; 3 and under free. Last tickets sold
½ hour before closing.

Welcome to one of the world's oldest zoos. Founded in 1793 during the French Revolution, it was created to house animals displaced from the royal menagerie at Versailles. It's the perfect scale for young children yet still fascinating for the entire family.

One of the zoo's current missions is to host lesser known and endangered species. Elephants, lions, bears, and larger animals have been moved from the zoo over the past two decades, shifting the focus to small and medium-sized species. That said, there are still crocodiles, giant tortoises, and a magnificent snow leopard. Parents and children will find it difficult to tear themselves away from the acrobatics of the orangutans housed in the art-deco style *singerie,* constructed in 1936. Try to stick around until 2pm–2:30pm when the zookeepers feed them. Older kids may be interested to know that in 1870, when Parisians were starving during the Prussian siege, many of the zoo animals were eaten.

Kenzo Tribouillard/AFP/Getty Images

Exiting Jussieu Métro station, notice the large windows on the
complex of university buildings that run along rue Jussieu. Zoo
entrances can be found off of rue Linné or rue Cuvier. The latter, via rue Jussieu, is the most direct entrance from the Jussieu
station. Just beyond the busy **La Baleine** café (see page 217)
inside the garden walls is a sign indicating the entrance to the
Ménagerie. A playground, a public **toilet**, a **snack stand**, and
picnic tables near the entrance make this a good stop to refuel
or regroup. Once inside this stroller-friendly zoo, there's another
casual **café** with kid-friendly items like sweet or savory crêpes,
hot dogs, pasta, and desserts (2,3€–8€). Tables are available for
packed picnic lunches as are a number of **restroom** facilities.

La Grande Galerie de l'Évolution

Inside Jardin des Plantes
36, rue Geoffroy-St-Hilaire, 5th arr.
01.40.79.54.48
www.mnhn.fr
Daily 10am–6pm; closed Tuesday
Adults 7€; free for under 26. Last tickets sold 45 minutes before closing. Baby-changing station on the ground floor, stroller-friendly.

The Grand Gallery is organized around three principal concepts: evolution, the biodiversity of animal and marine life, and endangered and extinct species from around the world. On the ground floor, visitors can explore marine life—be sure to see the skeleton of a blue whale. The next level is dominated by a long procession of animals that includes giraffes, elephants, and Louis XV's royal rhinoceros—it's an impressive demonstration of taxidermic skill. Mounted exhibits of endangered and extinct animals are displayed in a semi-darkened room on the second level (*niveau 2*). Helpful information cards in English are tucked into wooden benches scattered around the museum.

The museum's **café** overlooks the gallery; its menu features a club sandwich, bagels, a hot dog, pasta box, wok in a box, candy, muffins, brownies, and drinks (2,5€–8€).

La Galerie des Enfants

Inside La Grande Galerie de l'Évolution, Jardin des Plantes
Daily 10am–6pm; closed Tuesday; last entry at 5pm
Adults 9€; 4–26 years 7€; free for under 4 (includes entry to
Grande Galerie de l'Évolution)

Added to the natural history museum's permanent exhibits in
2010, the Galerie des Enfants is a bilingual, interactive exhibit
designed for children 6 to 12 years old. Visitors enter on a rotating
basis; tickets indicate the entrance time. The gallery explores the
concept of biodiversity while focusing on three themes: the city,
the river, and the Brazilian tropical forest.

Les Galeries de Paléontologie et d'Anatomie Comparée

Inside Jardin des Plantes
2, rue Buffon, place Valhubert, 5th arr.
01.40.79.56.01
www.mnhn.fr
Daily 10am–5pm; closed Tuesday
Adults 7€; free for under 26

Kids will like the dinosaur exhibits in this Paleontology museum;
adults will appreciate the fact that the museum has not been
modernized and retains much of its vintage character.

La Baleine

Inside Jardin des Plantes
47, rue Cuvier, 5th arr.
01.40.79.80.72
www.restaurant-la-baleine.com
Daily noon–3pm

La Baleine's spacious terrace bustles with children and toddlers, especially when the weather is fine. It works best for the *goûter* (snack) or for those with time to eat a leisurely meal. The menu changes seasonally; in warmer months it features a grilled vegetable salad, gazpacho, shrimp with fresh avocado in vinaigrette, and melon and ham (19€). The menu always includes items with broad appeal: hamburgers, fish, vegetarian salad, and curry (entrée + plat, 21€). The children's menu offers a choice of chicken nuggets with fries, pasta with salmon, or a cheeseburger with fries, choice of dessert, and a drink (11,90€).

Le Marché Monge

Place Monge, 5th arr.
M Place Monge
Wednesday and Friday 8am–1:30pm; Sunday 8am–2pm

Place Monge is a pleasant open-air market with around 40 merchants who sell produce and flea market wares such as clothing, household items, and other novelties. Prepared food from the market's Chinese take-out, the olive merchant, or the cheese stand make easy options for a picnic in one of the nearby parks. Marché Monge is a convenient option for those who want to experience the spirit of a flea market without having to brave the crowds and chaos of the large ones.

Musée National du Moyen Age

6, place Paul-Painlevé, 5th arr.

01.53.73.78.00

M Cluny-La Sorbonne

www.musee-moyenage.fr

Daily 9:15am–5:45pm; closed Tuesday; last tickets sold at 5:15pm
Adults 8,5€; 18–25 years 6,5€; free for under 18. Audio guides in
English 1€. Toilets with changing station downstairs from front desk.
Not a stroller-friendly museum. Best for 5 years and older.

Paris's museum of medieval art and artifacts is housed amidst
the ruins of the city's ancient Roman thermal bath complex. Two
exhibits may be of particular interest to children: the 15th-century
Lady and the Unicorn tapestries in Room 13, and the Heads of the
Kings of Judah in Room 8. Five of the six tapestries portray the
woman engaged in activities that symbolize the senses: sight, taste,
touch, hearing, and smell. The Heads of Judah gallery displays 21 of
the 28 original figures that once adorned the front of Notre Dame
Cathedral. In 1793, revolutionaries mistook these statues for French
kings and tore them down from the façade to discard as scrap. They
were rediscovered almost 200 years later buried in the courtyard of
a mansion in Paris's 9th arrondissement.

The museum's temporary exhibits are generally interesting to kids;
some programs have included a look at the use, symbol, and myth
of medieval swords, and cosmetics and skin care from Antiquity to
the Middle Ages. The museum organizes workshops, family visits,
and story time in French for children 0–12 years old.

Families will find a lovely playground shaded by the buildings of the
ancient Roman complex in the square de Cluny, off of boulevard

St-Germain between rue de Cluny and boulevard St-Michel. Like almost all of Paris's public playgrounds, its play structure sits on top of a cushioned surface. There are two sections, one for 3- to 10-year-olds and the other for 2- to 8-year-olds, as well as a free public **restroom** and drinking fountain. It is open daily 8am to sunset.

EAT

Also see Jardin des Plantes, page 217.

Amorino

16, rue de la Huchette, 5th arr.

01.43.54.73.64

M St-Michel; RER: St-Michel-Notre-Dame

www.amorino.com

Daily 11:30am–midnight

Gelato

This popular maker of gelato and sorbet has 22 locations in the capital. Created daily and locally, recipes are free from added coloring, preservatives, or artificial flavorings. There are usually a dozen or so flavors in the case: caramel with salted butter, pistachio, coffee, speculoos, vanilla, and dark chocolate among others. Portions are generous so be sure to ask for the Gelato Bimbo size for kids.

Breakfast in America (BIA)

17, rue des Écoles, 5th arr.

01.43.54.50.28

M Cardinal Lemoine, Jussieu

www.breakfast-in-america.com

Daily 8:30am–11pm with continuous food service

When BIA's founder Craig Carlson moved to Paris, the only thing he missed from home was a "good ol' American breakfast." To fill the niche, he opened this 1950s-style American diner complete with ketchup-red upholstery, vintage movie posters, a soda-fountain counter, and a bilingual staff. The diner offers American standards: breakfast burritos; banana, blueberry, or chocolate-chip pancakes; chicken nuggets; and cheese or chili-cheese fries. BIA is one of the few places in Paris that serves American-style bacon. For lunch and dinner there are classic burgers, salads, and desserts such as milk-shakes and ice cream floats (4,95€–8,95€).

Carrefour City Café
23, rue Linné, 5th arr.
01.55.43.02.61
M Jussieu
Monday–Saturday 7:30am–10pm; Sunday 10am–10pm
This convenience store on the corner of rue des Arènes and rue Linné, minutes from Jardin des Plantes and the Square Capitan playground, sells picnic-friendly foods, including a large selection of pre-packaged sandwiches, salads, juices, sodas, teas, fresh fruit, chips, candy, and ice cream (1€–3€). A self-service machine brews up espresso drinks in plastic cups.

Aux Cerises de Lutèce
86, rue Monge, 5th arr.
01.43.31.67.51
M Place Monge, Censier-Daubenton
Aux Cerises de Lutèce-Lili Feutrine Shop, Facebook page
Tuesday 10am–6:30pm; Wednesday–Saturday 10:30am–6:30pm
The dark green storefront of this adorable tea salon and curio shop wraps the corner of rue Monge and rue de l'Épée de Bois. It's only minutes from the Arènes de Lutèce and Jardin des Plantes. The menu is limited with about a dozen items each day, but the pastas,

quiches, tartines, and desserts are all carefully crafted and tasty
(lunch menus 9,5€–12€).

Gelati d'Alberto

45, rue Mouffetard, 5th arr.

01.77.11.44.55

M Place Monge, Censier-Daubenton

Gelati d'Alberto, Facebook page

Daily noon–midnight; hours vary in fall and winter

Gelato maker Alberto Afonso, native of Parma, Italy, recreates his
grandfather's secret gelato recipe in his two shops in the heart of
Paris. There are no artificial colors or preservatives in flavors like
Tarte Tatin, but you will find tiny pieces of fresh apple. Unusual
flavors such as wild *myrtille*, cinnamon-date, Paris-Brest, and salted-
butter caramel are offered alongside more traditional ones. Using
a spatula, servers carefully shape the gelato into petals that form a
rose on the top of the cone (2 flavors 3,5€; 3 flavors 4,5€; 4 flavors
5,5€).
Additional location: 12, rue des Lombards, 4th arr., **M** Châtelet.

Hippopotamus

9, rue Lagrange, 5th arr.

01.44.07.18.20

M Maubert-Mutualité

www.hippopotamus.fr

Sunday–Thursday 11:45am–11pm; Friday–Saturday 11:45am–
midnight (continuous food service)

Hippopotamus is a casual, family-friendly chain similar to Chili's
or Applebee's in the U.S. Late opening hours and continuous food

service make it a convenient option for jet-lagged families. Its bal-loon-decorated reception area and kids' coloring activities make the restaurant feel oddly familiar. Grilled meats are l'Hippo's specialty, but traditional French bistro items like steaks and salads are offered, as well as a handful of not-so-bistro-like burgers, fish sticks, chicken nuggets and wings (set menus 14,9€–20,9€; kids' menu 6,9€). Hippopotamus has more than 25 locations in Paris, but like any chain, each branch varies in service and quality; the locations listed here seem to be the most consistent.

Additional locations: 29, rue Berger, 1st arr., **M** Les Halles; 1, boulevard des Capucines, 2nd arr., **M** Opéra; 20, rue Quentin Bauchart, 8th arr., **M** George V; 12, avenue de Maine, 15th arr., **M** Montparnasse-Bienvenue.

Pâtisserie Viennoise

8, rue de l'École de Médecine, 6th arr.

01.43.26.60.48

M Odéon

Monday–Friday 9am to 7pm; closed Saturday and Sunday

Just off Boul'Mich, look down towards the end of this narrow street for the bakery's huge sign. Founded in 1928, the *pâtisserie* is popular with students from the medical school around the corner who appreciate strudel (2,9€), sacher tortes (3,2€), carrot cake (2,9€), coffee, and hot chocolate. Inexpensive lunch choices include pasta with cheese (7,5€), penne with chicken (7,5€), and fresh salads (7,5€). Dark wood, dim light, and tightly squeezed tables make this historic café-bakery abundantly charming, particularly welcoming on rainy days, but the interior is too small for strollers.

Sugarplum Cake Shop

68, rue du Cardinal Lemoine, 5th arr.

01.46.34.07.43

M Cardinal Lemoine

www.sugarplumcakeshop.com

Tuesday–Sunday noon–7pm

Not far from Arènes de Lutèce off of rue Mouffetard is a friendly bakeshop, established in 2010 by a group of three North Americans. It's a renovated space in an old building, swathed in light on sunny days and comfortably cozy on cooler ones. The kitchen serves up delicious homemade treats on a menu that changes daily and always includes cake. The shop's wedding cake business is thriving in fact, offering Parisians an alternative to the traditional inverted cone-shaped mound of cream puffs, the *croquembouche*, traditionally served at French weddings. Other menu items include melt-in-your-mouth chocolate-chip cookies; cupcakes in flavors such as chocolate, Oreo, or strawberry; pecan toffee squares; muffins; scones; and cinnamon rolls (2,5€–4,5€). To drink, choose among homemade lemonade, iced tea, fresh pressed juices, sweet syrups mixed with water, coffee, and an assortment of teas.

SHOP

Les Deux Tisserins
36, rue des Bernardins, 5th arr.
01.46.33.88.68
M Maubert-Mutualité
Toys

Nestled in between rue Monge and boulevard St-Germain, Les Deux Tisserins carries a variety of toys at reasonable prices: puzzles, books, arts and crafts sets, traditional wooden toys, dolls from French brands Corolle and Petitcollin, costumes, sand toys, marbles, balls, and ride-ons for kids. The shop also has a limited infant and toddler clothing section.

L'Épée de Bois
12, rue de l'Épée de Bois, 5th arr.
01.43.31.50.18
M Censier-Daubenton, Place Monge
Tuesday–Saturday 11am–7pm; Sunday 11am–1pm
Toys

With a superb selection of wooden toys and the virtual absence (or at least underrepresentation) of more mainstream brands, this Latin Quarter shop is a real find. Behind its vibrant green façade is a joyful interior filled with puppets, sand toys, French-brand Papo figurines, pinwheels, child-sized backpacks, and loads of wooden toys including many sizes of sailboats, perfect for the *bassins* in Luxembourg and Tuileries gardens (10" boat 14€, 12" x12" 43€).

Gibert Joseph

26–34, boulevard St-Michel, 6th arr.
01.44.41.88.88
M Cluny-La Sorbonne, Odéon
www.gibertjoseph.com
Monday–Saturday 10am–8pm
Books, Gifts

Four Gibert Joseph stores are grouped closely together here on boulevard St-Michel. The building at the corner of rue Racine and boulevard St-Michel, with "Papeterie" in huge yellow letters attached to an upper balcony, has countless choices for not-so-touristy souvenirs for children or young adults: ink pens, journals, notebooks, totes, pouches — many decorated with the monuments of Paris — and French school supplies.

Jouets Bass

8, rue de l'Abbé de l'Épée, 5th arr.
01.43.25.97.01
M Cluny-La Sorbonne; RER: Luxembourg, Port Royal
www.bassetbass.fr
Monday 2pm–7pm; Tuesday–Saturday 10:30am–7pm
Toys

Jouets Bass, and its sister store Galerie Bass located across the street at 7, rue de l'Abbé de l'Épée, are some of the best stops in Paris for wooden and other unique toys including replicas of Bauhaus games and toys, based on designs found in the Bauhaus archives in Berlin, by Naef. Behind the shops' bright blue storefronts, shoppers find a vast selection of wooden musical instruments, educational games, ride-ons, German-made wooden

figurines; smaller items like pinwheels, stuffed animals, spinning tops, music boxes, and puppets; and a variety of delightful boats perfect to launch in Jardin du Luxembourg's fountain. Aspiring knights can arm themselves with the shop's armor, shields, and swords, some made from wood, others from plastic or foam. Bass specializes in reproductions of old toys as well as sophisticated building games like Architekton, inspired by Russian artist Kasimir Malevich.

Kiria

108, boulevard St-Germain, 6th arr.

01.55.42.52.49

M Odéon

Kiria, Facebook page

Monday–Saturday 10am–8pm

Baby Gear

Kiria is a health and well-being store with a sizable baby-gear section on its ground floor. Parents can find a selection of umbrella strollers, larger buggies (prams), infant carriers, Stokke products, cloth diapers, and children's toys and books.

Shakespeare and Company

37, rue de la Bûcherie, 5th arr.

01.43.25.40.93

M St-Michel

www.shakespeareandcompany.com

Daily 10am–11pm; Saturday and Sunday 11am–11pm

Books

This iconic, Left Bank English bookstore has a small children's section upstairs. George Whitman, the shop's first owner, named it in honor of Sylvia Beach's fabled early-twentieth-century bookshop and lending library of the same name. Beach's Shakespeare and Company became a cultural and intellectual center for the Anglo-American literary set in Paris—James Joyce, Hemingway and Fitzgerald were regulars. (Whitman's daughter, Sylvia, now owns and manages the shop.)

George Whitman's bookstore was popular with Beat generation writers such as Burroughs and Ginsberg and it continues to be a magnet for contemporary writers and other artists. Aspiring authors might like to know that "Hotel Tumbleweed," Whitman's nickname for the shop's overnight enterprise, still operates inside. Residents, mostly writers, trade work in the bookstore for a free place to sleep at night; improvised beds are assembled in nooks, aisles, on book display stands, or wherever possible.

Tout Noté
35, rue Jussieu, 5th arr.
01.43.25.28.24
M Jussieu
www.toutnote.fr
Monday–Saturday 10:30am–7:30pm; Sunday 3–7pm
Stationery, Gifts

Tout Noté is a surprisingly large *papeterie*, filled with colorful, whimsical paper goods and other novelties. Close to the Jardin des Plantes, the boutique provides a wide range of thoughtfully selected alternatives to the typical Parisian souvenir: journals, totes, photo albums, pencil pouches, cards, decorative items, keepsake boxes, and hanging paper mobiles, many decorated with illustrations of Paris and its monuments. You'll also find unusual items such as Do Not Forget doorknob organizers, a yellow submarine tea ball, and more.

STAY

Hôtel Résidence Henri IV

50, rue des Bernardins, 5th arr.
01.44.41.31.81
M Maubert-Mutualité
www.residencehenri4.com/index.php
Elevator/AC/Wifi
Doubles from 145€; apartments from 250€

A charming, independent apartment-hotel, the Henri IV is a find for families. Tucked into a quiet cul-de-sac adjacent to Square Paul Langevin, a quiet park with a playground for 2- to 10-year-olds, the location couldn't be better. In addition to eight guest rooms, there are five apartments that sleep up to four people; all of them have kitchenettes with a small refrigerator, mini-bar, electric cooktop, microwave, dishes, and utensils. Rooms are traditionally decorated and uniquely themed, recalling King Henri IV and significant personalities in his life.

PLAY

EAT

SHOP

STAY

St-Germain-des-Prés

PLAY

Les Catacombes de Paris
1, avenue du Colonel Henri Rol-Tanguy, 14th arr.
Place Denfert-Rochereau
01.43.22.47.63
M Denfert-Rochereau
www.catacombes.paris.fr
Tuesday–Sunday 10am–5pm; last entrance at 4pm
Adults 8€; 14–26 years 4€; 13 and under free
Audio guides available in English: 3€ (30-minute commentary)
Best for children 10 and older

The 45- to 90-minute (2km) walk through Paris's underground ossuary is best limited to parents and teenagers. It's dark, damp, and with the remains of around 6,000,000 Parisians, it's downright creepy. Only 200 visitors are permitted to wander this labyrinth of bones at a time; waits can be long in summer. It's about 55–60 degrees (F) underground and there are no restroom facilities — prepare accordingly. An audio or tour guide makes this walk more interesting than a self-guided visit. Once a month Paris Walks, a company that organizes a number of walking tours in English around the capitol, takes visitors through the Catacombes. The commentary is always riveting and humorous. The group meets at the Catacombes' entrance by Denfert-Rochereau (adults 21€, which includes the Catacombes entrance fee; 14–16 years 19€; 13 and under free. Reserve and prepay in advance by cash or credit card. Paris Walks, 01.48.09.21.40, www.paris-walks.com).

Jardin du Luxembourg

Entrances off place Edmond Rostand, place André Honnorat, rue Guynemer, rue d'Assas and rue de Vaugirard, 6th arr.
www.senat.fr/visite/jardin
Between 7:30am and 8:15am–sunset; hours vary with season

Luxembourg Garden is quintessential Paris with children; generations of families have strolled, played, and picnicked in this storied park. It's the kind of place that tempts parents to consider relocating to Paris. Le Luco, as it is affectionately called by Parisians, makes visitors feel like locals. Its elegant landscape is a paradise for kids: an elaborate playground, an enclosed marionette theatre, Charles Garnier's vintage carousel, pony and donkey rides, and model sailboats in the grand *bassin* make it easy to idealize life in the capital.

Many of the activities are clustered on the western side of the park, closest to the rue Guynemer and rue d'Assas entrances. The majority of them charge a small fee, so bring cash. Children love the pony rides, pedal-powered cars, and swings (1,5€–2,5€). There are, however, free public sandboxes just south of the Orangerie and on hot summer days the wading pools, also free, are filled with water. The **Buvette des Marionnettes du Jardin du Luxembourg** is a café-snack bar that serves tartines, salads, ice cream, and candies. **Le Pavillon de la Fontaine** on the opposite side of the park also offers café-type fare and has lots of outdoor seating. Within the garden are a handful of kiosks that sell drinks, treats, and small toys. Most of the lawns are off-limits, but three, close to rue Auguste-Comte, are open for picnics and play on alternate days. If there's no space on the grass, it usually isn't difficult to find space on one of the 3,500 park benches or nearly 5,000 armchairs scattered throughout the park. The Kiosque à Musique, on the park's eastern side, hosts free concerts in spring, summer, and fall (schedule available on website).

Le Poussin Vert

Inside Jardin du Luxembourg, 6th arr.

Closest entrance: rue Guynemer or rue d'Assas

10am–7pm; hours vary with season

Adults 1,20€; children 2,50€; discounted multiple-entry pass available. No credit cards.

This vast playground is comprised of two zones, one for kids 7 years and younger, a second for 7- to 12-year-olds. On busy days it can be downright wild, too overwhelming for young or timid children. The possibilities for play however, are limitless: jungle gyms, tunnels, slides, seesaws, a sandbox, spinners, and a zip line (cableway) keep kids moving. **Restrooms** and a **snack bar**, stocked with candies, ice cream, popsicles in summer, and espresso for parents, are available inside the play area.

Marionettes, Théâtre du Luxembourg

Inside Luxembourg Garden, 6th arr.
Closest entrance: rue Guynemer; near the Poussin Vert playground
01.43.26.46.47
guignolduluxembourg.monsite-orange.fr
Performances Wednesdays, Saturdays, Sundays, holidays, and school vacations. Shows are usually at 11am and 3:15pm, but times vary; see website for individual performances.
Adults and children 4,5€

Robert Desarthis founded this theatre in 1933; today his son Francis-Claude continues the tradition of *guignol*, or puppet, theater. Performances are in French, but children of all ages will enjoy the characters' antics as they perform both familiar and traditional French tales.

Model Sailboats

Inside Luxembourg Garden, 6th arr.
Near the Grand Basin in the center of the garden
Weekends, Wednesdays, and during school vacations

For a few euros, toy sailboats may be rented and launched in the Grand Bassin. The children prod and guide the little vessels with wooden sticks, watching as the wind catches their sails and they swerve around the fountain.

Carousel

Inside Luxembourg Garden, 6th arr.
Near the Poussin Vert playground and the marionette theater
1,5 €

Charles Garnier, the architect of Paris's famous opera house, also designed the garden's irresistibly charming carousel (*manège*). Riders can try their skill at capturing a small ring with a baton provided by the carousel's operator.

Restrooms are available inside and just outside of le Poussin Vert playground, downstairs at the tennis kiosk (.40€). There are **restrooms** with a diaper-changing station and child-sized toilets near the Sénat buildlings at the Chalet de la Roseraie (.20€–.40€). There are two more public **restrooms** on the opposite side of the park.

Square Boucicaut

1, rue Babylone, 7th arr.
M Sèvres-Babylone
www.paris.fr
Daily sunrise to sunset

Neighborhood families and visitors alike, adore this playground at the intersection of rue de Sèvres and rue de Babylone, just outside of Le Bon Marché. Named after the department store's founder, the park has an engaging play structure for 2- to 8-year-olds and a separate area with a shorter slide and spring riders for younger ones. There's a **toilet** *cabine* just outside of the park's fence in one corner; **restrooms** inside of the department store are close enough to reach in an emergency.

Tour Montparnasse

33, avenue du Maine, 15th arr.

01.45.38.52.56

M Montparnasse-Bienvenue

www.tourmontparnasse56.com

Adults 7€; 16–20 years 4€; 7–15 years 3€; free for under 7

April–September 9:30am–11:30pm; October–March: Monday–Thursday 9:30am–10:30pm; Friday, Saturday, and holidays 9:30am–11pm

For a 360-degree view of Paris, ascend 689 feet to the rooftop terrace of Tour Montparnasse, a great alternative to the Eiffel Tower for families with young children. Lines are rare and it's an equally exquisite view. Twenty-five elevators serve a group of different floors; the quickest—which also happens to be the fastest elevator in Europe—whisks passengers directly to the panoramic level on the 56th level in 38 seconds. It's a few more flights of stairs to the skyscraper's roof. Sunset is the best time to take in the view from Montparnasse–watch as Paris lights up before your eyes. The entrance is located by the orange awnings marked Tout Paris à 360°. The tower is situated in a shopping district; several low to mid-priced department stores such as Galeries Lafayette, C&A, and Tati are nearby.

Yoga Enfants–Melanie Yoga Fitness

A.P.E., 4, rue de Fleurus, 6th arr.
06.18.02.35.58
M St-Placide
www.yogaenfants.com
Weekend workshops are 10:30–11:30am, see website for exact dates.
20€ adult and child; 10€ each additional adult or child
A British expat teaches yoga classes in English and French for children (1 year and older) indoors or, during spring and summer months, in the Luxembourg Garden. Yoga mats are supplied or participants may bring their own.

EAT

L'Avant Comptoir

3, carrefour de l'Odéon, 6th arr.

01.44.27.07.97

M Odéon

www.hotel-paris-relais-saint-germain.com

Daily 11am–2am

Yves Camdeborde, one of Paris's most celebrated chefs, opened this narrow little hors d'oeuvres/tapas bar and crêperie next door to his wildly popular restaurant, Le Comptoir du Relais. With only standing room at the bar and a take-away window for crêpes and galettes, it's a potential option for picnic food en route to Luxembourg Garden. The specialties to-go here are savory galettes, sweet crêpes, and waffles, but inside, there are salads, dried sausages, sandwiches, charcuterie platters, and other goodies. Topping choices for galettes: egg, mozzarella, ham, beef, roast chicken, and artichokes (1,5€– 5,5€); crêpe with sugar (1,5€), with jelly (2,5€); plain waffles (2,5€), with sugar (2,8€).

Bagels & Brownies

12, rue Notre-Dame-des-Champs, 6th arr.

01.42.22.44.15

M St-Placide

Monday–Saturday 9am–6pm

Satisfy a craving in a store that prepares all of its baked goods on site: bagels, brownies, muffins, and cookies. It's a tiny shop with only six barstools at a counter and no bathroom; still, it's convenient for grabbing a snack on the way to nearby Luxembourg Garden.

About a dozen bagel sandwiches, named after American cities, are on the menu, or you can create your own (4,5€–7€).

Le Bar du Marché
75, rue de Seine, 6th arr.
01.43.26.55.15
M Saint-Germain-des-Prés
Daily 7:30am–2am
This lively café at the corner of rue de Seine and rue de Buci has a large terrace and offers several choices for children whose palates haven't quite acclimated to their new environment. Omelets, basic sandwiches, and hot dogs are served alongside refreshed café classics like croques monsieurs/madames, steak frites, and salads. Kids will enjoy the friendly waiters who look a bit like Super Mario Brothers characters in their signature coveralls. Parents will love the ambience and the outstanding people-watching vantage that this café, right in the heart of the bustling Buci market with its fishmongers, bakers, butchers, and their customers, affords.

City Crêpes
73, rue de Seine, 6th arr.
01.46.33.08.18
M Mabillon
Monday 11:30am–3pm; Tuesday–Sunday 11:30am–11pm
City Crêpes is a casual crêperie with friendly service that serves flavorful food at reasonable prices. The lunchtime menu has a choice of galette (savory crêpe), crêpe, and a drink (11€). The menu offers a variety of original creations: the "Big Apple" galette is filled with raclette, onions, cream, bacon, and tomatoes. Sweet crêpes are also

well represented; the crêpe with caramelized apples and vanilla ice cream is simple but delicious (7€–10€ à la carte).

Coffee Parisien
4, rue Princesse, 6th arr.
01.43.54.18.18
M Mabillon
Daily noon–midnight with continuous food service until 11:30pm
Mexican and American food is the highlight at this diner-style restaurant in the heart of Saint-Germain. It's hugely popular with locals — avoid peak mealtime when the restaurant can be too noisy and crowded for little ones. At other, calmer times, a generous banquette running the length of the restaurant provides comfortable seating for families. Coffee Parisien provides many options for children with a limited culinary repertoire: scrambled eggs with bacon, pancakes, quesadilla with guacamole, and burgers (8€–13,50€).

La Coupole
102, boulevard du Montparnasse, 14th arr.
01.43.20.14.20
M Vavin
www.lacoupole-paris.com
Daily 8:30am–12am; reservations can be made through the website.
With its impressive dome and spectacular art deco interior, La Coupole, a legendary symbol of Montparnasse, is still a brasserie to behold. La Coupole served artists such as Picasso, Joyce, Matisse, Henry Miller, Man Ray, and Josephine Baker. Gainsbourg dined with Birkin and Chagall celebrated his 73rd birthday here. White tablecloths and professional, vest-clad waiters in black bow ties lend an

air of formality, but there's definitely room for children and strollers on the semi-enclosed terrace. Tourist mains like a club sandwich and french fries appear on the menu alongside oysters, an impressive plateau de fruits de mer, roast chicken, and all the traditional bistro standards (children's menu 11€; prix fixe 28€–33,5€).

Da Pietro Pizzeria

12, rue Mabillon, 6th arr.
01.43.54.62.34
M Mabillon, Odéon
Tuesday–Sunday 10:30am–2:30pm, 7–11:30pm

An air of authenticity distinguishes this family-owned Italian restaurant, situated just south of boulevard St-Germain. The Marra family uses recipes that have been passed down through three generations to create some of the best pizzas and pastas on the Left Bank. The menu changes daily but always includes the standards: a four-cheese pizza, pizza Parma (with tomato, mozzarella, and Parma ham), lasagna, pasta carbonara, and salads (6€–18€).

Gérard Mulot

76, rue de Seine, 6th arr.
01.43.26.85.77
M Mabillon, Odéon
www.gerard-mulot.com
Daily 6:45am–8pm; closed Wednesday

It's difficult to ignore the scent of rich butter wafting from Gérard Mulot's award-winning pastry/chocolate/*traiteur* shop on rue de Seine. While he has been formally honored for his baguette and strawberry tarte, Mulot's cream-filled pastries, fruit tartes, and maca-

rons have also garnered an unwavering following. His spacious Left Bank shop stages a tempting pastry and *viennoiserie* case. There's also a display of savories: sandwiches, shrimp salad, celeri remoulade, ratatouille, pizzas, and quiches. Mulot is the classic place for a well-heeled Saint-Germain family to buy a cake for a special occasion, but it's also an ideal stop for visitors to pick up picnic provisions en route to Luxembourg Garden, only five minutes away. The process of settling up may be annoying for some: customers wait in line to order; after ordering they are handed a ticket; they take the ticket and get in line again at the cashier to pay, then go back to where they ordered to retrieve their food. Service can be spotty, but patience is richly rewarded here.

L'Heure Gourmande

22, passage Dauphine, 6th arr.

01.46.34.00.40

M Odéon

Daily 11:30am–7pm

This discreet tearoom occupies a tranquil courtyard only minutes from Pont Neuf and the Seine. The terrace is small, but it provides a contained area for children to stretch their legs if needed; inside, the ambience can be quiet and subdued. The menu is on the light side, with quiches, salads, and other typical salon de thé items. A menu of homemade sweets that changes daily makes it a perfect choice for the *goûter*: the chocolate tarte, apple-wild berry-cinnamon crumble, lemon meringue tarte, and cheesecake are all daintily displayed on a dessert table (6,5€–8€). Coffee, teas, and artisan hot chocolate are also served.

Léon de Bruxelles

131, boulevard St-Germain, 6th arr.

01.43.26.45.95

M Mabillon

www.leon-de-bruxelles.fr

Sunday–Thursday 11:30am–12am; Friday, Saturday, and holidays 11:30am–1am

Léon de Bruxelles specializes in mussels and french fries, but there's also steak and a smattering of other seafood mains on the menu. Its nine locations remain a Parisian family favorite. Kids receive a game or coloring activity on arrival and some locations have play areas. Parents with infants and toddlers will find high chairs (a rarity in Paris), booster seats and, at some locations, diaper-changing amenities. The 6€–9€ kids' menu has choices of fish and chips, mussels, beef patty (*steak haché*), fish sticks, or chicken nuggets as well as a choice of drink and dessert.

Additional locations: 120, rue Rambuteau, 1st arr., **M** Les Halles; 63, avenue des Champs-Élysées, 8th arr., **M** George V.

Lili's Brownies Café

35, rue du Dragon, 6th arr.

01.45.49.25.03

M Saint-Sulpice, Sèvres-Babylone

Monday–Saturday 10am–7pm

It's easy to walk past this tiny bake, sandwich, and salad shop, located only a few blocks from the Square Boucicaut playground next to Le Bon Marché department store — but, if you're en route, it's worth a stop. The homemade goods are fresh: delectable cakes in flavors like chocolate-cherry and lemon-almond, as well as

American-style cookies, muffins, and brownies. The *fromage blanc*, served with honey and nuts, is a favorite among regulars (2€–7€).

Lina's Sandwich

22, rue des Sts-Pères, 7th arr.
01.40.20.42.78
M Saint-Germain-des-Prés
www.linassaintsperes.fr
Monday–Friday 9am–5pm; Saturday 10am–5pm

There's more than enough space for young children and strollers inside this location of the Paris-based international chain. Lina's menu has something for any child who likes a sandwich: ham and cheese, pastrami, tuna salad, turkey, and dozens of other choices. Some kids may find sandwiches in a typical Parisian café—made with a baguette, butter, ham, and cheese—too thick or crusty. Lina's offers a choice of white (*pain de mie*) or wheat loaf bread for its made-to-order sandwiches. The set lunch menu (12€) lets customers choose a sandwich, dessert, and drink. For breakfast, there are pastries, rolls, fresh fruit salad, yogurt, a bacon-and-egg or smoked salmon sandwich, and hot drinks. If it's a take-out kind of day, two minutes away is a small playground for 2- to 6-year-olds in Square Taras Chevtchenko, where rue des Sts-Pères and boulevard St-Germain meet.

Additional locations: 50, rue Étienne Marcel, 2nd arr., M Étienne Marcel; 61, rue Pierre Charron, 8th arr., M George V; 17, boulevard Malesherbes, 8th arr., M Madeleine.

Mamie Gâteaux

66, rue du Cherche-Midi, 6th arr.
01.42.22.32.15
M Sèvres-Babylone
www.mamie-gateaux.com
Tuesday–Saturday 11:30am–6pm; lunch served 11:30am–2:30pm

Mamie Gâteaux is a tearoom and café, owned by a Franco-Japanese couple, with the comfortable, familiar feel of grandma's house. It's busy with children and families who come to enjoy the homemade sweets: apricot-lemon cake, seasonal fruit tartes, pain perdu made with brioche, cream puffs, or molten chocolate cake. Pastry chef Mariko Duplessis trained at Dalloyau in Tokyo and at the Cordon Bleu after she arrived in Paris. On the lunch menu, which changes daily, is classic tearoom fare: savory tartes, fresh salads, and soups made from scratch (4€–8,5€).

PDG

5, rue du Dragon, 6th arr.
01.45.48.94.40
M Saint-Germain-des-Prés
www.pdg-rivedroite.com
Daily 12:30–2:30pm, 7:30–10:30pm

PDG was born when French restaurateur Pierre Lannadère decided to open a "true American restaurant" in the Saint-Germain-des-Prés neighborhood. It can be pricey, but service is friendly, and ingredients are fresh and French; the hamburger buns are created by one of the top bakers in France. Although compact, the restaurant's rear seating area provides ample room for kids. On the menu are steak tartare, hamburgers, hot dogs, cheeseburgers made with goat cheese, club sandwiches, fries, and generous salads; the plate of mini-burgers works well for kids (12,5€–21€). Brunch (adults 28,5€, children 15€) is served on weekends: pancakes with maple syrup, scrambled eggs and bacon. Check PDG's website and Facebook page for discounts and specials.

SHOP

Alice à Paris

9, rue de l'Odéon, 6th arr.
01.42.22.53.89
M Odéon, Luxembourg
www.aliceaparis.com
Monday 2pm–7pm; Tuesday–Saturday 11am–7pm
Clothes

This independent Parisian designer with three boutiques in the city creates simple, classically cut styles in traditional colors for kids one month to 10 years old. Most of the clothing is made in Tunisia, which keeps prices lower than expected for designer apparel. Soft pants and wide-cut peasant blouses are especially comfortable at school or on the playground.

Additional locations: 64, rue Condorcet, 9th arr., **M** Anvers; 11, rue de l'Annonciation, 16th arr., **M** Boulainvilliers.

Bonpoint

6, rue de Tournon, 6th arr.
01.40.51.98.20
M Odéon
www.bonpoint.com
Monday–Saturday 10am–7pm
Clothes

Bonpoint successfully marketed what has become the quintessential look for effortlessly chic Parisian children when it opened its first boutique in 1975. The style is classic, refined and — its designers and sales staff insist — playground-appropriate and worthy. A point of reference, inspiring scores of French children's fashion labels, Bonpoint is also regarded as the epitome of a style against which edgier designers have reacted and ultimately rebelled.

The sparkle of an elaborate chandelier dominates the white, relatively spartan entrance of Bonpoint's flagship store on rue Tournon. Once inside, a wooden playhouse welcomes kids to play while the impossibly cute clothing displays bring warmth to the boutique. Seasonal lines for girls 0 to 18 and boys 0 to 14 years old feature traditional colors like muted lavenders and grays, small flower prints, and plaids. Shoppers will find Bonpoint's full range here: formalwear with fun, sparkly options for girls, toys, shoes, and its own brand of perfume and skincare for children. Nursery furniture and baby paraphernalia from other labels are also stocked. Bonpoint has an online store and several locations in the U.S.

Downstairs, **Café Bonpoint** serves a light tearoom-style menu in a kid-friendly, modern-rustic space. When the weather is fine, the splendid, private courtyard opens for service (lunch 25€; *goûter* 10€; Tuesday–Saturday 10am–6pm).

Le Bon Marché

24, rue de Sèvres, 7th arr.
01.44.39.80.00
M Sèvres-Babylone
www.lebonmarche.com
Monday–Saturday 10am–8pm; Thursdays and Fridays until 9pm
Clothes, Toys, Books, Gifts

La Grande Épicerie de Paris

38, rue de Sèvres, 7th arr.
01.44.39.81.00
M Sèvres-Babylone
www.lagrandeepicerie.fr
Monday–Saturday 8:30am–9pm
Food

Le Bon Marché on Paris's Left Bank is one of the world's oldest — it celebrated its 160th anniversary in 2012 — and most elegant department stores. The soaring space, designed in part by Gustave Eiffel's architecture firm, has an air of luxury and refinement — and this *grand magasin* doesn't usually see the heavy tourist traffic of stores like Galeries Lafayette and Printemps on the Right Bank. Several sections are of particular interest to parents with kids; the store's basement floor has expansive departments for children's clothing, toys, books, and crafts and a more limited section for baby gear. Infant changing stations can be found in the store's restrooms on levels -1 and 3. Adjacent to the department store is La Grande Épicerie de Paris, Le Bon Marché's massive international supermarket and food hall. Four **café-restaurants**, suitable for kids while not being overly child-friendly, are available within the two buildings.

Le Bon Marché is an excellent bet for parents with little time and a long shopping list; prices are comparable to boutiques and Paris's other *grands magasins*. A cave of wonders for kids, the toy department is stocked with the best in French and international toy and craft brands — my daughters have happily whiled away hours leafing through books, scooting around on ride-ons, and snuggling stuffed animals. The clothing section is populated with expensive labels like

Bonpoint, Burberry, and Baby Dior; it's an expedient one-stop over-view of children's couture and high-end brands. Shoppers will also find a small department with nursery furniture, linens, decorative items, umbrella strollers, buggies, infant carriers, and feeding accessories.

When parents want to shop for themselves, my family's strategy involves one of us heading to the store to shop while the other accompanies the kids to Square Boucicaut, a playground at the intersection of rue de Sèvres and rue de Babylone, just outside of the department store (see page 240). It's heartening to know that a smorgasbord of **take-away** options awaits families just two minutes away inside La Grande Épicerie: French, Chinese, Italian, Japanese, even American prepared dishes that the staff will heat up for you to take back to the park, with utensils and napkins provided. It's also a grocery store with good picnic choices: yogurt, cheese, beverages, sandwich fixings, and an elaborate pastry and bread section. In short, La Grande Épicerie offers one of the most exquisite selections in the capital for whatever you or your children might be craving.

Les Cousins d'Alice
36, rue Daguerre, 14th arr.
01.43.20.24.86
M Denfert-Rochereau
Tuesday–Saturday 10am–7:15pm; Sunday 11am–1pm
Books, Toys
Murals of Alice, the Cheshire cat, and the story's other characters decorate the façade of this whimsical book and toy shop at the corner of rue Lalande and rue Daguerre, a few blocks from the Catacombes de Paris. Inside, shelves are densely stacked with

books, puppets, toys, puzzles, and lots of cuddle-worthy *doudous* (lovies). Small tables provide space for little ones to sit comfortably and look through beautifully illustrated books.

Du Pareil Au Même (DPAM)

168, boulevard St-Germain, 6th arr.
01.46.33.87.85
M Saint-Germain-des-Prés
www.dpam.com
Monday–Saturday 10am–7pm
Clothes, Shoes

DPAM offers an appealing selection of both understated French children's fashions in muted colors along with more modern, brightly colored styles. DPAM's prices are affordable, usually better than Monoprix. Some branches specialize in shoes or baby gear, others limit themselves to clothing. Clothes for children 0–14 years old are sold in 36 Parisian boutiques.

Il Était une Fois

1, rue Cassette, 6th arr.
01.45.48.21.10
M Saint-Sulpice
www.neminemo.com
Monday–Saturday 10am–7:30pm
Toys

An entrance reminiscent of a funhouse tunnel leads shoppers into this basement-level, Saint-Germain toy boutique. Once inside, they find a space brimming with children's favorites: bicycles, ride-ons, dollhouses and accessories, Petitcollin dolls, board games, puzzles, and snuggly infant toys. The choice of Papo figurines and accessories is extensive: knights, princesses, animals, wooden castles, forts, and pirate ships. Costumes and toys for older children are upstairs. The shop is 5 to 10 minutes from the Luxembourg Garden so if you're in need of sand toys, it's an easy walk.

Marie Puce
60, rue du Cherche-Midi, 6th arr.
01.45.48.30.09
M Sèvres Babylone, St-Placide
www.mariepuce.com
Monday 1:30–7pm; Tuesday–Saturday 10:30am–2pm, 2:30–7pm
Clothes

Marie Puce's only retail boutique is located on a bustling stretch of rue du Cherche-Midi. Two sisters teamed up in 2003 to design timeless styles in wearable fabrics for infants, boys, and girls 0 to 18 years old. Colors range from delicate to bold and many of the girls' lines incorporate delightfully cheery prints from Liberty fabrics. Marie Puce's clothes, most of them manufactured in France, are also available for purchase from their e-shop.

Mille Fêtes

26, rue de l'Abbé Grégoire, 6th arr.

01.42.22.09.43

M Sèvres-Babylone, Rennes

www.millefetes.com

Monday 1–7pm; Tuesday–Friday 10:30am–7pm; Saturday 10:30am–1pm, 2–7pm

Party Supplies, Costumes

Mille Fêtes is made up of two boutiques located just minutes apart from one another. The party supply and costume store, tucked away on rue de l'Abbé Grégoire, carries a substantial collection of difficult-to-find party goods. A helpful staff delights in assisting customers

find party favors, accessories, cake decorations, candles, confetti, piñatas, or colorful tableware. Creative, made-to-order balloon arrangements are the owner's passion.

Mille Fêtes
60, rue du Cherche-Midi, 6th arr.
01.42.22.09.43
M Sèvres-Babylone, Rennes
www.millefetes.com
Tuesday–Saturday 10:30am–7pm
Toys
Treasures fill every nook in this bright and cheerful toy store on rue

du Cherche-Midi. A gracious shopkeeper helps the steady stream of locals find the perfect gift. Mille Fêtes specializes in wooden toys and equipment for outdoor activities: roller blades, tricycles, kites, jump ropes, and gardening and sand toys. Kids will be thrilled with the generous stock of figurines, stuffed animals, infant lovies, stickers, music boxes, wooden boats, and pirate toys.

Monoprix

50, rue de Rennes, 6th arr.
01.45.48.18.08
M Saint-Germain-des Prés
www.monoprix.fr
Monday–Saturday 9am–10pm
Clothes, Baby Care, Snacks

This branch of Monoprix is a large, centrally located one-stop shop for babies and children. Head downstairs to find groceries, infant and children's clothes, and a section with baby care and feeding items. Gear is limited to essentials such as lightweight umbrella strollers and baby carriers. This location has an aisle with inexpensive arts and crafts supplies, party-favor-sized toys, and infant favorites such as Sophie la Giraffe and mini Corolle dolls. The modern **café** downstairs features an 11€ prix-fixe menu and table service. Shoppers are tempted with salads, cheese platters, sandwiches, and quiches in a more casual self-serve area adjacent to the café. **Restroom** facilities are nearby.

My Sweet Bio

8, rue de l'Odéon, 6th arr.
01.43.26.39.60
www.mysweetbio.fr
M Odéon
Monday 1–7pm; Tuesday–Saturday 10:30am–7pm
Organic Clothes, Baby Gear, Skin Care

My Sweet Bio is one of the rare, all-organic, eco-conscious, comprehensive baby boutiques in Paris. The shop has been well supported in this neighborhood of expats and its English-speaking staff is attentive and knowledgeable. There's much more than meets the eye in this diminutive space; toys, bibs, bottles, nursing clothes and accessories, disposable and reusable diapers, wipes, and the entire range of Stokke products are available as well as organic makeup, perfume, and skin and hair care products for adults and children. French designers are emphasized in the selection of organic clothing, and My Sweet Bio recently launched its own line of clothes that includes layette basics, most of them made to order by a local seamstress. Sizes range from newborn to 8 years. Upstairs is a treatment room for skin care services and prenatal, postnatal, and infant massage (40€–70€).

Natalys

74–76, rue de Seine, 6th arr.
01.46.33.46.48
M Mabillon
www.natalys.com
Monday–Saturday 10am–7pm
Clothes, Baby Gear

Conveniently located on rue de Seine near Luxembourg Garden is one of Natalys's nine Parisian stores. Parents can find a full range of infant products: strollers, cribs, baby furniture, buntings, toys, portable high chairs, car seats, UV-protected tents for a park or beach outing, bottle and food preparation items, maternity clothes, and the brand's own line of mid-range layette wear. Oh — and this being France — there's of course a perfume line for infants, toddlers, and children.

L'Oiseau de Paradis

211, boulevard St-Germain, 6th arr.
01.45.48.97.90
M Rue du Bac
www.loiseaudeparadis.fr
Monday 2:30–7pm; Tuesday–Saturday 10:30am–7:30pm
Toys

L'Oiseau de Paradis has been in the toy business since 1932. It sells everything from artisan to mass-produced toys: Playmobil, Lego, costumes, Barbie dolls, wooden boats, vintage-style ride-ons, puzzles, educational games, and infant toys. Of the three Paris locations, the Saint-Germain store is the most agreeable and has the largest selection.
Additional locations: 86, rue Monge, 5th arr., **M** Censier-Daubenton, Place Monge; 96, avenue Mozart, 16th arr., **M** Jasmin.

Pom d'Api

28, rue du Four, 6th arr.

01.45.48.39.31

M Saint-Germain-des-Prés

www.pomdapi.fr

Monday–Saturday 10am–7pm

Shoes

Expect noticeably well-crafted shoes in a wide range of styles for infants and children at Pom d'Api. Located near the corner of rue du Four and rue Bonaparte, south of boulevard St-Germain, is one of this third-generation shoemaker's four Parisian boutiques. Pom d'Api's history hasn't interfered with its ability to stay fresh; you'll find everything from the most conservative shoes to modern, playful styles in metallics and bright colors. The colorful Nelson Marshmallow sofa beckons to children to take a seat while a staff member swoops in for an efficient measure and fitting. Pom d'Api is available internationally, but the best selection is still in France. Additional location: 13, rue du Jour, 1st arr., M Les Halles.

Serendipity

81–83, rue du Cherche-Midi, 6th arr.

01.40.46.01.15

M Sèvres Babylone, St-Placide

www.serendipity.fr

Tuesday–Saturday 11am–7pm

Furniture, Décor, Toys

Serendipity is an eclectic design boutique with a carefully selected blend of vintage and modern furnishings and decorative items for children's rooms. The designers have found plenty of space to offer

Courtesy of Serendipity

Courtesy of Serendipity

Courtesy of Serendipity

Courtesy of Serendipity

a collection of limited edition and one-of-a-kind objects as well as their own creatively refurbished pieces in a renovated 2000-square-foot garage in the Saint-Germain district. Serendipity's e-shop gives a good overview of its range of quirky products such as a child's lounging bed made from a net and filled with soft foam balls that conform to the shape of the body, minimalist stuffed animals, découpaged birdhouses, and mushroom night lights.

Talc vêtements
40, rue Jacob, 6th arr.
01.42.77.52.63
M Odéon
www.talcboutique.com
Monday 2–7pm; Tuesday–Saturday 11am–7pm
Clothes

The independent label Talc brings a modern, minimalist edge to basics for infants 3 to 18 months and children 2 to 12 years old. The color palette is simple: grays, black, shades of white, light and dark denim, red, and khaki. Talc's collections usually include variations of smock-style dresses, tunics, pea coats, and blazers—French classics.

Tati

68, avenue du Maine, 14th arr.
01.56.80.06.80
M Gaîté
www.tati.fr
Monday–Saturday 10am–7:30pm
Clothes, Accessories, Household Items

Shoppers in search of elusive rock-bottom prices in Paris head to Tati. Nothing groundbreaking fashion-wise, but Tati's essentials wear quite nicely for play and travel; think Monoprix, only less stylish and less expensive. Tati stores carry household items and adult clothing as well.

STAY

Hôtel du Danube
58, rue Jacob, 6th arr.
01.42.60.34.70
M Saint-Germain-des-Prés
www.hoteldanube.fr
Elevator/AC (in all rooms except standard)/Wifi
Apartments from 250€

Three-star Hôtel du Danube is 10 minutes by foot from both the Musée du Louvre and Musée d'Orsay. The quality of the rooms varies, ranging from recently remodeled *contemporaine* to relatively tired standard. Five apartments that sleep up to four people are offered for families (250€). Some of the superior rooms have space for a rollaway bed for children under 12 (30€); over 12 years of age, 50€. Infant cribs are available upon request at no charge. Special pricing is given when families book adjacent rooms—the second is discounted. Although smoking is forbidden in public areas of the hotel, none of the guest rooms are designated as exclusively non-smoking so there may be residual odor from previous guests; feel free to check out your assigned room before accepting it.

Hôtel Luxembourg Parc
42, rue de Vaugirard, 6th arr.
01.53.10.36.50
M St-Sulpice, Mabillon
www.luxembourg-paris-hotel.com
Elevator/AC/Wifi

Doubles from 250€

Ideally situated directly across from the Luxembourg Garden, this elegant boutique hotel has top-notch amenities in an unrivaled location for families with young children. Executive rooms and the junior suite sleep two adults, one child under 12, and an infant under 2 years old with an extra bed and crib (250€–550€). The comfortable library, bright patio, and cheerful breakfast room distinguish this boutique hotel and offer guests a bit of extra space.

Hôtel Relais St. Germain

9, carrefour de l'Odéon, 6th arr.
01.44.27.07.97
M Odéon
www.hotel-paris-relais-saint-germain.com
Elevator/AC/Wifi
Doubles from 400€

Relais St. Germain is no secret. Rooms book up four to five months in advance in this 4-star hotel adored by anglophones. Reserve early to find space in this inviting, beautifully decorated, and centrally located hotel owned and managed by acclaimed chef Yves Camdeborde and his wife, Claudine. Each room is larger than average for Paris — doubles can accommodate families of four on a king-sized bed and day bed with trundle (400€). A gourmet breakfast is included in the price of the room and can be taken in-room at any time during the day or until 10:30am in the restaurant. Extra beds are available (50€), as are baby cots.

Hôtel le Sénat

10, rue de Vaugirard, 6th arr.

01.43.54.54.54

M Odéon

www.hotelsenat.com

Elevator/AC/Wifi

Doubles from 195€; suites from 285€

Hôtel le Sénat is steps away from one of Paris's best parks for families, the Jardin du Luxembourg. The hotel is refined yet unassuming; its location off of the main street gives guests the sense of living in a Parisian neighborhood while still being in the central city. Individual rooms are compact, but Hôtel le Sénat is one of the few boutique hotels to have true connecting guest rooms. Deluxe rooms can sleep up to three people (from 195€); the large suites on the 5th and 6th floors can accommodate two adults and two children (from 285€). Modern décor, comfortable beds, and amenities such as flatscreen TVs, individually controlled air conditioning, and Hermès toiletries, as well as the helpful, bilingual staff, make le Sénat a solid choice.

La Villa Saint Germain

29, rue Jacob, 6th arr.

01.43.26.60.00

M Saint-Germain-des-Prés

www.hotelvillasaintgermain.com

Elevator/AC/Wifi

Doubles from 156€

This 4-star hotel enjoys a stellar location between the Seine and the church of St-Germain-des-Prés. It's remarkably calm and well-priced for such an exclusive and convenient location. The Junior Suite can accommodate up to two adults and two children (280€ + 50€ per extra bed/night). A branch of Ladurée, known globally for its pastries and macarons, is located directly across the street—the minty, gray-green colored façade is unmistakeable.

Additional hotels for families in the 6th arrondissement:

Hôtel de l'Abbaye
10, rue Cassette, 6th arr., 01.45.44.38.11,
www.hotelabbayeparis.com, **M** Saint-Sulpice.
Duplex Apartment for four from 500€.

Hôtel d'Angleterre
44, rue Jacob, 6th arr., 01.42.60.34.72,
www.hotel-angleterre-paris.net, **M** Saint-Germain-des Prés.
Suite for four from 300€.

PLAY

EAT

SHOP

STAY

Musée d'Orsay

PLAY

Hôtel National des Invalides

129, rue de Grenelle, 7th arr.
08.10.11.33.99
M Invalides, La Tour-Maubourg, Varenne
www.invalides.org
Daily 10am–6pm, Tuesday until 9pm (April–September); 10am–5pm
(October–March); closed the first Monday of each month
Adults 9€; free for under 18
Best for children 10 years and older

King Louis XIV commissioned the construction of Les Invalides, a
residence and hospital for injured soldiers, in 1670. A portion of the
massive complex continues to function as a veterans' hospital while
much of it serves as a military museum. Napoleon's tomb rests
under one of Paris's most visible landmarks, the golden dome. The
inner courtyard, flanked by historic cannons, is still used for official
military ceremonies.

The Musée de l'Armée chronicles France's military from the 13th
century to modern times. Children interested in military history may
enjoy seeing the vast collection of authentic uniforms and how they
varied geographically and between each branch. The World War II
rooms trace the evolution of the conflict from its inception to reso-
lution. Parents may find a few of the images depicting the carnage
of war in paintings and period film footage to be too graphic for
young children.

Visitors will find the **cafeteria** near the complex's southern entrance, not far from Napoleon's tomb. It offers a child-friendly menu (quiches, lasagna, sandwiches, hot dogs and various snacks, desserts, and soft-serve ice cream) in a casual, self-service setting.

Le Musée des Égouts de Paris
Entrance opposite 93, quai d'Orsay by Pont Alma, 7th arr.
01.53.68.27.81
M Alma-Marceau; RER: Pont de l'Alma
www.paris.fr
October–April, Saturday–Wednesday 11am–4pm; May–September closes at 5pm; closed Thursday and Friday. Adults 4,30€; 6–16 years 3,5€; free for under 6. English tours in summer.
Best for children 7 years and older

A one-hour visit takes tourists to a section of Paris's network of sewers, through the labyrinth of tunnels that forms a city beneath the city. The self-guided tour begins with a stop in a small museum and a short film on Paris's sanitation system. Visitors then head out to see first-hand how the system works — how water is processed and cleaned in the capital. It's not for the faint of heart; tourists cross a river of raw sewage en route; the odor is sufficiently foul, but not overwhelming for most. Stop by the souvenir booth for a plush sewer rat to remember the experience. Sparkling-clean **restroom** facilities await visitors just beyond.

Musée National Rodin

Hôtel Biron, 79, rue de Varenne, 7th arr.
01.44.18.61.10
M Varenne
www.musee-rodin.fr
Tuesday–Sunday 10am–5:45pm; closed Monday
Adults 6€; 18–25 5€; free for under 18; family (2 adults and children under 18) 10€; admission to the garden only, 1€
Audio guides with commentary in English prepared specifically for families with children 6 to 12 years old; 3€ for one child and one adult; 1,5€ for each extra audio guide

Many of Rodin's best-known works are displayed in Hôtel Biron, the elegant mansion where the artist once lived and worked, and its gardens. The sculptor's studies on the human form in the museum's interior galleries are captivating even for young children. The highlight, however, is the garden where they can run and play among the artist's sculptures. Little ones recognize the contemplative expression on the face of *Le Penseur* and love to imitate his pose. My children were embarrassed by the nude sculptures, such as *Adam* or *Jean d'Aires nu*, that seemed to stand over them at every turn, but it gave us a chance to talk about art and the human body. Our highbrow discussions, however, didn't impede their game of hide and seek. The outdoor space is also a quiet haven with meandering paths and peaceful corners, ideal for strolling with a slumbering child.

The **Café du Musée Rodin** is situated within the museum's garden. In good weather, the roomy terrace is a relaxing setting for lunch or afternoon tea; the interior of the greenhouse-inspired café also has seating. Mains include soup, healthy salads, savory tartes, sandwiches, and a daily special (5,5€–10,5€). The menu provides snack options as well: cakes, muffins, yogurt, fruit salad, and ice cream. Garden **restrooms** are close to the café.

Musée d'Orsay

1, rue de la Légion d'Honneur, 7th arr.
01.40.49.48.14
M Solférino; RER: Musée d'Orsay
www.musee-orsay.fr
Daily 9:30am to 6pm, Thursday until 9:45pm; closed Monday
Adults 8€; 18–25 5,5€; free for under 18
Stroller-friendly, baby-changing station on level D1; high chairs in restaurant.

Children typically enjoy the Musée d'Orsay, not only when they find out about the building's history — it's a former train station — but also for the famous pieces from artists that they may recognize: van Gogh, Manet, Renoir, Dégas, Toulouse-Lautrec, and many others. The bright, spacious quality of the sculpture gallery, the tremendous, iron-framed ceiling, and the huge clock in this museum are breathtaking at any age. Its collection of paintings, sculptures, drawings, photography, and objets d'art date from 1848 to 1914. In the fall of 2011, after major renovations, the Musée d'Orsay unveiled a new

look and layout in many of its gallery rooms. If traveling with children younger than 7 years old, 60 to 90 minutes should be ample time for a quick look at the sculpture hall and a visit to the Impressionist and Post-Impressionist galleries plus time for snack, meal, and/or restroom break.

To minimize frustration, avoid Sundays and Tuesdays, which are usually the museum's busiest days, or visit in the morning or on Thursday evenings when it's open late. Choosing the correct entrance will reduce idle queue time. Entrance A is used for individuals without (advance) tickets; Entrance C, with shorter lines, serves visitors with tickets or museum passes and those with priority entry (pregnant women, disabled visitors, students, members, press). Those who buy tickets online through the Orsay's website have access to entrance C. These tickets are not available for pickup at the museum, but must be printed at home or collected at FNAC media retail stores around Paris.

The color, texture, and generally pleasant subject matter of the art exhibited in the Impressionist galleries on Level 5 (*niveau supérieur*), located primarily in gallery rooms 29 to 36, is almost always appealing to children. Highlights include: Renoir's *Bal du Moulin de la Galette* (room 32) and *Jeunes Filles au Piano* (room 36); Monet's series of Rouen Cathedral paintings (room 36) and water lily canvases (room 36); and Manet's *Le déjeuner sur l'herbe* (room 29), which may inspire some entertaining questions. Many young girls are drawn to Degas's paintings of ballerinas: *Répétition d'un ballet sur la scène* (room 31), the *Danseuses bleues* (room 36), and *La classe de danse* (room 36), as well as his upward-gazing, tutu-clad sculpture *Petite danseuse de quatorze ans* (room 31). Van Gogh's *Starry*

Night, a self-portrait, and other paintings are displayed on level 2 (*niveau médian*) in rooms 71 and 72, as is the work of Gauguin (room 70), Seurat (room 69), and other Post-Impressionists.

The interactive floor plan on the museum's website is an easy way to plan a visit. Users enter the name of an artist, work of art, or keyword and a list of pertinent work that is currently on display appears. Visitors can skim the cursor over a title and immediately see where it's located within the museum on the interactive map. With one click, the title will be added to the *trail* (itinerary), as it's called on the site. The itinerary is saved under *My selection*, then *Planning your visit*, on the English website. Visitors can see and print the compiled list of the works that have been saved along with their exact location within the Musée d'Orsay.

Family visits and thematic hands-on workshops are organized in French for kids 5 to 18 years old. The schedule can be accessed through the French version of the museum's website. From the main page, select the *Visite* tab, then the *Visiteurs individuels* tab; *Visites jeune public* lists guided tours with workshops that may include painting, drawing, dancing, or acting for 5- to 10-year-olds as well as more sophisticated themes for adolescents (visit/workshop: 2 hours, 7€). Guided family tours with child-centered themes such as Home Sweet Home, A Look at Childhood, When Art Tells Stories, and Major Works from the Musée d'Orsay are regularly organized; more can be found under the *Visites en famille* section also under the *Visiteurs Individuels* tab (1½ hours, 4,5€).

There are four choices for food at the museum:

Café Campana

Located just beyond the Impressionist Gallery
Tuesday–Sunday 10am–5pm; Thursday 10am–9pm
Café Campana offers a Parisian brasserie menu (salads,
pastas, croques, and pastries) as well as stir-fried dishes and
an unforgettable view of the clock (12€–18€).

Restaurant du Musée d'Orsay

First floor
01.45.49.47.03
Tuesday–Sunday 9:30am–5:45pm; Thursday 9:30am–
2:45pm, 7–9pm
Sparkling chandeliers hang beneath the sumptuously
painted ceiling of this period dining room. The luxury belies
a relatively affordable, seasonal menu of traditional French
cuisine that is interspersed with more creative dishes
(arugula with tomatoes, artichokes and Buffalo mozzarella,
shrimp tempura served with crunchy vegetables, steak tartare, roasted fish with organic vegetables, pork filet mignon
with herbs and pan-fried gnocchi, grilled sirloin steak with
fries, plat du jour; à la carte 25€; set menu 16,5€; children's
menu 6,7€). Afternoon tea is served between 2:45 and
5:45pm.

Café du Lion

At the entrance to the museum, near the base of the large clock
Tuesday–Thursday 9:30am–5pm; Thursday until 8pm
A self-service café with light selections: soup, sandwiches, desserts, and drinks.

Boutique du Parvis

On the museum's plaza
Tuesday–Sunday 10am–5:30pm
This take-away stand sells sandwiches, snacks, crêpes, waffles, and drinks to go.

Also see Musée d'Orsay, page 286.

Le Bac à Glaces

109, rue du Bac, 7th arr.
01.45.48.87.65
M Rue du Bac
www.bacaglaces.com
Monday–Friday 11am–7pm; Saturday 11am–7:30pm

After school the line of children and parents at Le Bac à Glaces' take-away window stretches to the end of the block. The demand speaks volumes about the quality of the artisanal sorbet and ice

Alison Harris

cream made inside this neighborhood institution. Around 20 flavors are available in cones or cups at the to-go window. Inside this vintage ice cream parlor à la Parisienne, customers cozy up around eight tables to find additional classic and creative flavors, elaborate sundaes, and sweet treats (4,5€–8€). At lunchtime savory tartes, salads, and a daily special are served (13,5€–15€).

La Pâtisserie des Rêves
93, rue du Bac, 7th arr.
01.42.84.00.82
M Rue du Bac, Sèvres-Babylone
lapatisseriedesreves.com
Tuesday–Saturday 9am–8pm; Sunday 9am–4pm
This dreamy pâtisserie, five minutes from Le Bon Marché department store, is known for its decadent Paris-Brest pastry. Glass cloches suspended from the ceiling cover fancy cakes and seasonal tartes on a large, round table in the center of the boutique. A pain au chocolat, an éclair, or a fruit tarte are perfect to take a few blocks away and enjoy in the Square des Missions Étrangères park and **playground** at 105–107, rue du Bac, 7th arr., where there's a sandbox and play equipment for 2- to 8-year-olds. Travelers feeling nostalgic for a less modernized Paris, can find a free, albeit rustic (i.e., squat toilet) public **WC** in the square.

SHOP

Bleu comme Gris

99, rue du Bac, 7th arr.

09.53.32.14.81

M Rue du Bac

www.bleucommegris.com

Monday–Saturday 11am–7pm

Clothes

Dissatisfied with her daughter's outdated school uniform, Vanessa Marrapodi decided to modernize the tired frocks of French school-children and designed her own collection. Her styles were a hit with parents and administrators; it wasn't long before some of Paris's most exclusive private schools approached her with interest. Clients were enamored with Marrapodi's aesthetic and flooded her with requests for weekend wear that embodied the same spirit as her uniforms. The result is a collection of simple, fun, and comfortable styles in colorful fabrics. The small boutique carries shoes, knitted pieces, and accessories for children 6 months to 16 years old. The collection of uniforms, including the timeless, loose-fitting *tabliers*, or school smocks, may be seen online. Don't miss the *Look* tab on the store's site — more than two dozen ensembles offer inspiration for complete, head-to-toe looks for your mini-sartorialist with hats, scarves, shoes, and accessories.

Bonpoint (Fin de Série)

42, rue de l'Université, 7th arr.

01.40.20.10.55

M Rue du Bac

www.bonpoint.com

Monday–Saturday 10am–7pm

Clothes, Shoes, Accessories

Bonpoint has a handful of boutiques clustered together on rue de l'Université near the intersection of rue du Bac. This outlet location offers entry-level prices on the luxury brand; prices on the previous season's collection of clothes and accessories for children 0–16 years are discounted 30%–40%. After customers have made their selection from the samples on hangers, the staff is happy to look for sizes in the meticulously folded stacks of clothes. The shop is less crowded during school hours.

A white façade indicates the nearby Bonpoint Naissance shop (67, rue de l'Université), dedicated to clothing and accessories for newborns 0 to 3 months. Next door, also at #67, is Bonpoint Enfant, a separate boutique for children up to 12 years old, and Bonpoint Chaussures, at #65, carries shoes. The building at #86 has two boutiques, YAM, Bonpoint's line designed for tweens, teens, and petite mothers, and Bonpoint Garçon, which specializes in boys' clothing.

Bonton

82, rue de Grenelle, 7th arr.
01.44.39.09.20
M Rue du Bac
www.bonton.fr
Monday–Saturday 10am–7pm

The label has three adjacent boutiques on rue de Grenelle that share the same store hours.

The largest of the cluster is an enormous loft-like space where parents can find clothing for kids 12 months to 12 years old or look through the tables of quirky, fun gifts. Bébé Bonton has items for infants 0–12 months and Papillon offers higher-end clothing in finer, more expensive fabrics.

Another branch of Bonton that carries contemporary nursery furniture, bedroom linens, Japanese-inspired and imported novelties, children's books, and party goods, is located three minutes away from the rue de Grenelle group of stores on rue du Bac. Bonton Bazar, 122, rue du Bac, 7th arr., 01.42.22.77.69, **M** Rue du Bac, Monday–Saturday 10am–7pm.

Noro

4–6, rue de Varenne, 7th arr.
01.45.49.19.88
M Rue du Bac
www.noroparis.com
Monday–Saturday 11am–7pm
Clothes

The dreamy colors in Noro's children's boutique are reminiscent of a Renoir painting. The collections, made in France, are characterized by fine fabrics and a palette of white, gray, navy, and old rose. Designers also sell a small selection of scarves, hats, and other accessories. Noro recently collaborated with Monoprix to produce a less expensive line for the ubiquitous French chain.

Rose & Theo

80, rue du Bac, 7th arr.
01.45.44.58.83
M Rue du Bac
www.rosetheo.fr
Monday–Saturday 10:30am–7:30pm
Clothes

A sparkling chandelier illuminates the boho chic décor of this petite boutique. Rose & Theo began with a line of bathing suits in 2003, and has since expanded to offer complete seasonal collections for infants 3 to 18 months, girls 2 to 12 years old, and boys to 10 years. The clothes are elegant, adorable, and made abroad, which allows Rose & Theo to offer a lower price point than other small labels. Kids' school totes, shoes, headbands, and other accessories are also sold in the shop.

Tartine et Chocolat

266, boulevard St-Germain, 7th arr.

01.45.56.10.45

M Solférino

www.tartine-et-chocolat.fr

Monday–Saturday 10am–7pm

Clothes

Tartine & Chocolat's Saint-Germain boutique, located across from the Ministry of Defense, occupies two large connected retail spaces. Styles trend toward formal—a look most appropriate and practical for a luncheon or dressy play date; prices are on par with higher-end children's boutiques; the staff also tends to be formal. Tartine & Chocolat produces a perfume and skin-care line for infants and an eau de parfum for children 3 years and older. The French label also sells a full range of nursery furniture, linens, décor, accessories, and luxurious stuffed animals.

Additional locations: 24, rue de la Paix, 2nd arr., **M** Opéra; 84, rue du Faubourg St-Honoré, 8th arr., **M** Saint-Phillipe-du-Roule; 60, avenue Paul Doumer, 16th arr., **M** Trocadéro; 142, rue de Courcelles, 17th arr., **M** Wagram.

Hôtel d'Orsay

93, rue de Lille, 7th arr.

01.47.05.85.54

M Musée d'Orsay

www.paris-hotel-orsay.com

AC/Elevator/Wifi

Doubles from from 160€; suites from 225€

Hôtel d'Orsay is well located on a quiet street mere blocks from the Musée d'Orsay. A few minutes' walk from the hotel is a pedestrian footbridge, the Passerelle de Solférino, that connects the Orsay area with the Tuileries garden on the opposite side of the river. Families will find the hotel's 540-square-foot junior suite that sleeps up to four people and a crib, well-appointed and comparatively spacious for Paris (from 225€). The Supérieure guest rooms will most comfortably accommodate an infant bed (from 160€). One concern for families with Hôtel d'Orsay is that its neighbors are primarily government and commercial offices — cafés and grocery stores aren't immediately convenient.

PLAY

EAT

SHOP

STAY

Tour Eiffel

PLAY

The American Library in Paris
10, rue du Général Camou, 7th arr.
01.53.59.12.60
M Pont de l'Alma
www.americanlibraryinparis.org
September to June, Tuesday–Saturday 10am–7pm; Sunday 1–7pm;
reduced hours in July and August

Five minutes on foot from the Eiffel Tower is Continental Europe's
largest lending library of English-language books. The American
Library organizes a drop-in story circle each Wednesday for parents
and children. Additional themed readings and other activities in
English are planned each month for kids. Visitors must join the
library to participate — a week-long membership designed for tourists is available at 28€ for an individual or 39€ for a family. This
short-term pass doesn't allow borrowing privileges but does include
full access to the library's collections including newspapers and
magazines as well as unlimited Wifi access.

Bateaux Parisiens

Port de la Bourdonnais, 7th arr.

08.25.01.01.01

M Trocadéro

www.bateauxparisiens.com

Adults 12€; 3–12 years 5€; departures from Notre Dame: adults 12€; 3–12 years 6€; 2 and under free. Wednesday afternoon children's cruises depart at 2pm and 3:45pm; 2 years and older 12€.

Departure points are located near the Eiffel Tower (at Pier number three) or Notre Dame Cathedral (Quai de Montebello). Boats from Notre Dame have live commentary from a guide, while those from the Eiffel Tower have individual audio guides. The cruises include Paris's most important sights as they make the one-hour loop around Notre Dame Cathedral and the Seine islands on one end, and the Eiffel Tower at the other. Two elves tell the story of Paris through songs and games on *La Croisière Enchantée,* a cruise on Wednesday afternoons designed especially for children. Commentary is only in French but the characters make it entertaining for non-French speakers.

Les Cars Rouges

17, quai de Grenelle, 15th arr.

01.53.95.39.53

M Bir-Hakeim

www.carsrouges.com

Daily 9:30am–10:10pm depending on bus stop

Adults 26€; 4–12 years 13€; free for under 3. Tickets can be bought on the bus, in hotels, or online (10% discount when purchased on website).

These big red buses shuttle tourists between nine stops in central Paris (Eiffel Tower, Champ-de-Mars, Louvre, Notre Dame, Orsay, Opéra, Champs-Élysées-Étoile, Grand Palais, Trocadéro. The guided hop-on, hop-off tour takes 2 hours 15 minutes to follow the complete loop without stopping. Tickets are valid for two consecutive days.

Fat Tire Bike Tours

Meet at south pillar of Eiffel Tower, 7th arr.
01.56.58.10.54
M Bir-Hakeim
www.fattirebiketours.com
April 1–October 31, daily 11am and 3pm; November 1–March 31, 11am
Adults 28€; students 26€; trailers and tandem trailers are half the tour price for adults; baby seats are free.
A 4-hour bike tour takes participants to see sights that include the Eiffel Tower, Napoleon's Tomb, the Louvre, Musée d'Orsay, Tuileries Garden, and the Champs-Élysées. Baby seats, trailers, tandem trailers, small mountain bikes, and beach cruisers are available to reserve in advance for families with children. Tours to Versailles meet at the company's office near the Eiffel Tower (24, rue Edgar Faure, 15th arr., **M** Dupleix).

Pierre Verdy/AFP/Getty Images

Musée du Quai Branly

37, quai Branly, 7th arr.

01.56.61.70.00

M Alma-Marceau; RER: Pont de l'Alma

www.quaibranly.fr

Tuesday, Wednesday, Sunday 11am–7pm; Thursday, Friday, Saturday 11am–9pm

Adults 8,5€; free for under 18

Two audio guides are available in English, a 2-hour overview of the collections and a 45-minute family tour (5€, 2€ each additional; visitors can also download the guides in mp3 format from the website, 3€).

Opened in 2006, Musée du Quai Branly is one of Paris's newest museums. Approximately 3,500 items are organized by continent: Asia, Oceania, Africa, Antarctica, and the Americas. It's a good bet for budding anthropologists or for those interested in tribal cultures. The museum is a striking, modern structure surrounded by a jungle of vegetation. Once inside, visitors walk up a long, winding ramp to the exhibits, past nearly 9,000 musical instruments. The 45-minute family audio guide is particularly useful as bilingual signage isn't one of Quai Branly's fortes. Kids will find the collection of exotic art and artifacts intriguing: masks used in mystical ceremonies and war, weapons, jewelry, voodoo dolls, and ritualistic figures produced by indigenous peoples from around the world. Encourage your kids to notice the materials used to create the items: snakeskin, feathers, grizzly bear claws, animal horns, wood, leather, and seashells along with many others.

A discovery brochure is available online, along with a 2-hour self-guided tour of the museum's masterpieces (*Practical Museum* tab, *Suggestions for your visit*). The website's French version also has a booklet in French for children 7 to 12 years old; some of the puzzles and activities can be understood without translation. Wednesday afternoons and weekends, hands-on workshops in French are offered for families and children 3 to 12 years old. The schedule is available in English on the website under *Programming*, then *Workshops and Master Class*. English-speaking kids will enjoy some of the hands-on classes; in Security Blanket participants tie-dye soft fabric using plant dyes and salts; Secret Dolls teaches children about various materials used in making dolls such as pig teeth and spider's webs and gives them the chance to make their own; Ta

Moko Tattoos first considers Maori skin carving and pigmentation through photographs and tools on display in the museum, after which participants use ink to create their own designs (1½–2 hours, 6€–8€).

Quai Branly has two choices for hungry families; both venues have patios with spectacular views of the Eiffel Tower. **Le Café Branly** is a pleasant spot for breakfast, lunch, or afternoon tea with salads, warm mains, pastries, and cakes (12€, 9€–23€, 10€; children's menu 10€). **Les Ombres Restaurant** on the upper terrace of the museum boasts an incredible vantage from its windowed dining room. Lunch, tea, and dinner are served during traditional French dining hours: noon–2:30pm for lunch, 3pm–5pm for tea, and 7pm–11pm for dinner (reservations: 01.47.53.68.00, www.lesombres-restaurant. com).

Le Musée National de la Marine

17, place du Trocadéro, 16th arr.
01.53.65.69.69
M Trocadéro
www.musee-marine.fr
Daily 10am–6pm; closed Tuesday
Adults 7€; free for under 18

Trocadéro, the plaza and gardens across the Seine from the Eiffel Tower, is also the site of the Palais de Chaillot. The Palais, built in 1937 for the World's Fair, houses several museums: Le Musée de l'Homme (anthropology), La Cité de l'Architecture et du Patrimoine (architecture and French monuments), and Le Musée National de la Marine (naval museum). The latter is of most interest to children — or, at least to a child with a specialized interest in naval and mari-

time history, three centuries of which is chronicled through art in the museum. The scaled models of ships from every period of French naval history, including Louis XV's collection of miniature vessels once used to train naval engineers, are a treat for kids.

The modern **Café Carlu** inside the Architecture and French Monuments museum is a relatively affordable cafeteria-style affair with salads, sandwiches, savory tartes, a warm daily special, pastries, and smoothies on the menu. Carlu's terrace offers an unrivaled view of the Eiffel Tower that's worth checking out. (Daily 11am–7pm, Thursday until 9pm, closed Tuesday; 01.47.05.65.57, www.citechaillot.fr)

Parc André Citroën

2, rue Cauchy, 15th arr.

Access from quai André Citroën, rue Leblanc, rue St-Charles, rue de la Montagne-de-la-Fage

M Lourmel, Javel-André Citroën

www.paris.fr

Daily 9am–sunset

Citroën, the French car manufacturer, once had an important factory on this Seine-side property in the 15th arrondissement, now occupied by a vast, modern park. Unlike most public parks in the city, the green lawns in its center are open for sport, play, and picnics. The centerpiece of this green space is a computerized fountain whose

dozens of water jets dance in a delightful, coordinated pattern. On hot days, visitors arrive dressed in bathing suits and splash about in the cool water, completely ignoring the posted *interdit* (prohibited) signs.

Ballon de Paris

Inside Parc André Citroën
01.44.26.20.00
www.ballondeparis.com
Daily, 9am until one-half hour before park's closing, weather permitting.
Weekends and holidays, adults 12€, otherwise 10€; 12–17 years 10€, otherwise 9€; 3–11 years 6€, otherwise 5€; free for under 3.
This gigantic hot air balloon, tethered to the ground within Parc André Citroën, can take 30 adults or 60 children almost 500 feet up in the air. If weather is questionable, check the website to verify that the balloon is running. Since 2008, the hot air balloon has also served as a pollution indicator to Parisians—when it's green, air quality is good, when it's orange, the quality is mediocre, and when red, poor.

La Tour Eiffel

Champ-de-Mars, 7th arr.
01.44.11.23.23
M Bir-Hakeim, Trocadéro; RER: Champ-de-Mars-Tour Eiffel
www.tour-eiffel.fr
Daily 9:30am–11pm; 9am–midnight (June 17–August 28)
Floor 2 via elevator: adults 8,50€; 12–24 7€; 4–11 4€; free for under 4
Top via elevator: adults 14€; 12–24 12,50€; 4–11 9,50€; free for under 4
Floor 2 via stairs: adults 5€; 12–24 3,50€; 4–11 3€; free for under 4
Strollers are permitted but must be folded in elevators; baby-changing facilities in restrooms.

The Eiffel Tower is the international symbol of France and, with more than 7 million visitors each year, *la Dame de Fer* (the Iron Lady) is also one of the world's most visited monuments. The funny thing about seeing the tower with children is that they—at least mine—aren't necessarily impressed. Sure, it's enormous; sure, it's an unforgettable silhouette against the Parisian cityscape; and, yes, even a toddler will be able to identify it after only a few glimpses. But don't take for granted the seemingly obvious appeal of the tower. Poor timing (i.e., tired or hungry kids), and the Eiffel Tower's allure begins to fade. Lines can be prohibitively long in summer without advance tickets, and it's not just the queues on the ground that are interminable: lines to take the elevator to the summit from the second floor can also be 1–2 hours.

It takes planning to pull off a pleasant ascent with kids and, fortunately, the tower's website provides everything a parent could want. Probably most important, advance tickets are available for purchase (to the second and top floors via elevator), substantially cutting what can be a painfully long wait in peak season. The tickets may be printed at home, downloaded to a mobile phone, or sent by mail. After visitors select a date, the site returns with a choice of available entrance times that begin every half hour. As with most pre-paid tickets, they are non-refundable, non-exchangeable, and non-transferable, terms that might prompt hesitation in the parents of infants and toddlers whose schedules have been disrupted by jet lag.

Some children may express a fear of heights at the thought of ascending to the top of the tower. Assure them that everything is enclosed and that there's no danger. Once you've arrived at level 2, move towards the summit elevators; lines for the elevators here can be quite long. Bring snacks and take your kids to the restroom beforehand; you don't want to lose your spot especially if you've spent time waiting. Even on warm days, it can be cool and windy at the top, so dress accordingly. Once you've made it to the summit, the view of Paris is dazzling; it's an exhilarating moment for the entire family. An undeniably cool spectacle, even for tired kids, is the Eiffel Tower's sparkling lights that are illuminated after night falls for five minutes at the top of the hour. In winter an ice-skating rink, open to those visiting the tower, is set up on the first floor (10:30am–10:30pm; equipment provided free of charge; personal skates not permitted).

The *Children's Tower* tab on the website's main English page has a downloadable bilingual booklet, intended for 6- to 10-year-olds, called *Follow Gus.* A trail of fluorescent-yellow footprints scattered around the tower's first floor leads to panels with stories, figures, and facts about the Eiffel Tower—all of the information they'll need to play the games and answer the questions in the booklet. Parents can use it to prepare their younger kids for their visit and let older ones hunt for the answers once they've ascended.

An abbreviated list of facts for young children: the tower was built in 1889 by Gustave Eiffel for the World's Fair to celebrate the 100th anniversary of the French Revolution; Eiffel had a weather station placed on the top—since then the tower's summit has also been used to broadcast radio and television signals; the tower is repainted every seven years—since 1968 it's been an undisclosed shade of bronze. Three tones of the color are used—the lightest is applied to the summit and the darkest to the tower's base.

There are three options for food at the Eiffel Tower (www.restauronts-toureiffel.comwww.restaurants). From 11:30am–4:30pm, the first-floor **58 Tour Eiffel**, a casual restaurant with a brasserie menu, offers a *pique nique* without reservation. Customers order drinks from a server then bring a picnic basket to the counter where they select and collect the cold portion of their meal (adults 18€, 2–11 years 11€). A prix-fixe dinner is served during two seatings, at 6:30pm and 9pm (adults 67€–150€, 2–11 years 14€–35€). **Jules Verne**, on the second floor, is a more formal setting with lunch and dinner menus ranging from 85€ to 200€; it can be accessed by a private elevator from the southern pillar. **Snack bars** on the first and second floors serve meals and snacks: salads, sandwiches, hot dogs, pizza, pastries, and ice cream. The tower's top floor also has a **champagne bar** where parents can celebrate the fact that they've made it up *en famille*!

The Champ-de-Mars is a vast public green space that runs from the Eiffel Tower to École Militaire. It's a children's paradise with puppet shows, go-carts, pony rides, a hand-cranked carousel, swings, several elaborate playgrounds, and picnic-friendly lawns. Les Marionnettes du Champ de Mars is a covered theater with shows Monday, Saturday, and Sunday at 3:15pm and 4:15pm (avenue du Général Marguerite, guignolduchampdemars.centerblog.net) 3,5€. Nearby is the **La Bonbonnière de Marie**, rue de Belgrade, 7th arr., a lovely, often overlooked café that serves salads, crêpes, snacks, and sweets in the Champ-de-Mars.

EAT

Also see Musée du Quai Branly, page 306.
Also see Tour Eiffel, page 313.

Amorino

42, rue Cler, 7th arr.
09 50 79 33 93
M École Militaire
www.amorino.com
Monday–Thursday noon–11pm; Friday–Sunday noon–midnight

This popular gelato and sorbet maker, Amorino, has 22 locations in the capital. Traditional Italian gelato is created daily and locally; recipes are free from added coloring, preservatives, or flavorings. There are usually a dozen or so flavors in the case: caramel with salted butter, pistachio, coffee, speculoos, vanilla, and dark chocolate among others; customers can choose as many as they wish. Portions are generous so be sure to ask for the Gelato Bimbo size for kids.

There are many branches of Amorino throughout Paris; some centrally located alternate locations include: 47, rue St-Louis en l'Île, 4th arr., **M** Pont Marie; 4, rue de Buci, 6th arr., **M** Odéon, St-Michel; 31, rue Vieille du Temple, 4th arr., **M** St-Paul; 18, rue Mouffetard, 5th arr., **M** Place Monge.

Cojean

19, rue Clément Marot, 8th arr.
01.47.20.44.10
M Alma-Marceau
www.cojean.fr
Monday–Friday 8:30am–5pm; Saturday 10am–5pm

Cojean is a small French chain of counter-service cafés specializing in healthy fast food. Its popularity has garnered international attention—Cojean was profiled in *Time* magazine as Paris's original "anti-fast food" eatery. Indeed, it filled a void in a lunch scene that once limited Parisians to omelets or steak frites and equally unimaginative sandwiches. Cojean has a large selection of salads, sandwiches, and vegetarian selections. Soup, grilled sandwiches, and hot mains such as lasagna or quiche change frequently and are noted on the chalkboard (6€–9€). Cojean also offers a variety of fresh-squeezed or creative fruit and vegetable juices.

Courtesy of Cojean

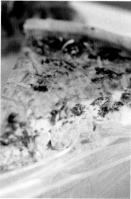
Courtesy of Cojean

Courtesy of Cojean

Additional locations: 3, place du Louvre, 1st arr., **M** Louvre-Rivoli; 17, boulevard Haussmann, 9th arr., **M** Chaussée d'Antin-La Fayette; 121, rue Réamur, 2nd arr., **M** Bourse; 6, rue de Sèze, **M** Madeleine; Printemps Mode, étage -1, 64, boulevard Haussmann, 9th arr., **M** Havre-Caumartin.

Martine Lambert

39, rue Cler, 7th arr.
01.45.51.25.30
M Ecole Militaire
www.martine-lambert.com
Wednesday–Sunday 10am–2pm, 3–7:30pm; Sunday 10am–2pm
Martine Lambert's culinary efforts began in Normandy, a region known for its rich dairy products. Lambert's *glaciers* (ice cream makers) create sorbets and ice cream to take away, in flavors that capitalize on France's best regional products: Cassis (blackcurrant) from Bourgogne, Framboise (raspberry) from Perigord, and Pomme (apple) from Normandy.

SHOP

Happy Garden
116, rue La Fontaine, 16th arr.
M Michel-Ange-Auteuil
01.40.50.06.67
www.happygarden.fr
Monday 2–7pm; Tuesday–Saturday 10:30am–7pm
Clothes

Indie-label Happy Garden brings a lighthearted, spirited perspective to children's fashion. Fabrics include cotton prints from the celebrated British brand Liberty, French-made organic bamboo jersey, and Italian wool. Happy Garden's website is a source of ideas; creatively styled ensembles under the *Looks* tab will inspire delight. The boutique also offers a sampling of small furniture, soft and wooden toys, decorative items, linens, and accessories.

Additional locations: 95, rue de Seine, 6th arr., **M** Odéon; Printemps Haussmann, 64, boulevard Haussmann, 9th arr., **M** Havre-Caumartin; 11 bis, avenue Victor Hugo, 16th arr., **M** Charles de Gaulle-Étoile; 215, rue du Faubourg St-Honoré, 8th arr., **M** Ternes.

Numaé

155, rue de Grenelle, 7th arr.
01.47.05.16.96
M La Tour-Maubourg, École Militaire
www.numae.fr
Monday–Saturday 10:30am–7pm
Clothes

This small, independent boutique just off of rue Cler is full of lovely choices for clothes and accessories for infants and children 0 to 4 years old. The hues are soft and classic, the fabrics luxurious: old rose, grays, crisp white, taupe, pale blues, and soft pinks, spun into

effortlessly chic styles. The shop has an excellent choice of nursery linens, soft shoes for pre-walkers, toiletry bags for kids, hats, gloves, diaper bags, plush animals, and a complete selection for baby's layette.

Additional location: 73, rue des Vignes, 16th arr., **M** La Muette, Boulainvilliers.

Soeur

5, rue Pierre Guérin, 16th arr.
M Michel-Ange-Auteuil
01.45.25.73.04
www.soeur-online.com
Monday–Saturday 10:30am–7pm
Clothes

Soeur makes it easy for parents to help their tweens fashionably bridge what can be the awkward transition between childhood and adolescence. The boutique, situated between Saint-Sulpice and the Jardin du Luxembourg, was created by two sisters in 2008. Domitille Brion spent 10 years as a designer at Bonpoint and co-created the Bonton label; Angélique, with a background in child and family psychology, directs marketing for the brand.

Soeur focuses on clothing for girls 10 to 14 years old, but also offers a selection for girls as young as 4 and as old as 16. The Brion sisters have seamlessly blended modern style with the charm, elegance, and naïveté of French children's fabrics and designs. The shop also carries accessories such as sunglasses, casual jewelry, fragrances, and scarves.

Additional location: 88, rue Bonaparte, 6th arr., **M** Saint-Sulpice

STAY

Hôtel la Bourdonnais

111–113, avenue de la Bourdonnais, 7th arr.

01.47.05.45.42

M École Militaire

www.hotellabourdonnaisparis.com

AC/Elevator/Wifi

Triples from 130€

Ten minutes from the Eiffel Tower and less than five from the playgrounds at Champ-de-Mars, Hôtel de la Bourdonnais is one of the rare hotels to offer affordable larger rooms and family-breakfast rates. La Bourdonnais has triples, quads, and a junior suite with two double beds and a living room area that can accommodate up to four people and an infant, for families of varying size (from 130€/150€/165€). Convenient to cafés, grocery stores, and Paris's top sights, Hôtel la Bourdonnais is a find for families.

Hôtel Duquesne Eiffel

23, avenue Duquesne, 7th arr.

01.44.42.09.09

M École Militaire

www.duquesneeiffel.com

AC/Elevator/Wifi

Doubles from 142€; triples from 208€

This charming hotel is located in a historic 18th-century building, a 10-minute walk from the Champ-de-Mars park and playgrounds and 20 minutes from the base of the Eiffel Tower. A 3-star hotel, Hotel

Duquesne has comfortable beds, an English-speaking staff, and great views of the tower from the fourth and fifth floors. Three classes of rooms with a double or Queen bed are offered: Standard, Confort, and Supérieure, the latter being the largest. Triples can accommodate three people, infants included (from 208€); connecting rooms in the standard and confort classes are also available for families (from 142€ per room).

Hôtel Muguet

11, rue Chevert, 7th arr.
01.47.05.05.93
M École Militare
www.hotelparismuguet.com
AC/Elevator/Wifi
Doubles from 135€; triples from 190€

If you're looking for a calm, elegant spot with a helpful, English-speaking staff close to the Eiffel Tower, look no further. Hôtel Muguet is situated in the middle of a residential neighborhood just 10 minutes by foot to Paris's most famous monument; visitors in rooms 52, 53, 61, and 62, however, can enjoy a splendid view of the Iron Lady without ever leaving the hotel. Muguet's 43 plain but clean and comfortable guest rooms were renovated in 2006. Doubles can accommodate a baby cot, available upon request; triples can be configured as one queen bed with a single tucked into a small alcove within the room, or three twin beds, and also have room for a baby bed.

Hôtel Relais Bosquet

19, rue du Champ de Mars, 7th arr.

01.47.05.25.45

M École Militaire

www.hotel-relaisbosquet-paris.com

AC/Elevator/Wifi

Doubles from 135€

Nestled into the rue Cler neighborhood, but off of the main thoroughfare, this boutique hotel is close to the Eiffel Tower and the child-friendly open spaces of the Champ-de-Mars. A copious breakfast buffet and self-service ice machine speak to the fact that the hotel's clientele is primarily American. Rooms are clean, cheerful, and well-appointed and there are grocery stores nearby. Superior rooms, at around 250 square feet, can accommodate two adults and one child in an extra bed (from 170€); infant cribs are available at no additional charge upon request. While there are no rooms that connect by interior doors, there are those with doors that face each other off of a tiny private hallway that can be made private with a third locking door (from 135€ per room).

PLAY

EAT

SHOP

STAY

Arc de Triomphe &
Champs-Élysées

Arc de Triomphe

Place Charles de Gaulle, 8th arr.

01.55.37.73.77

M Charles de Gaulle-Étoile

arc-de-triomphe.monuments-nationaux.fr

Daily 10am–11pm, April–September; 10am–10:30pm, October–March

Adults 9,5€; free for under 18

Elevator access to the middle level; restrooms inside the monument

Napoleon's Triumphal Arch, the Arc de Triomphe, was built in tribute to the French military and inaugurated in 1836. The names of 174 battles and the generals who participated in them are engraved inside the arch. Underneath, at the tomb of the unknown soldier, an eternal flame burns in honor of those who died in World War I. If your child is already a history buff, take a look at the incredible period newsreels of the WWII Victory parade after the liberation of Paris available on youtube and elsewhere online. The Arc de Triomphe stands majestically in the background as Allied troops march down the Champs-Élysées. For most children, the most fascinating part of the visit is the climb up the 284 steps to the top terrace and, from there, the impressive view of the city and the 12 avenues that radiate from the place Charles de Gaulle.

Bateaux Mouches

Port de la Conférence, Pont de l'Alma (on the right bank), 8th arr.

01.42.25.96.10

M Alma-Marceau

www.bateaux-mouches.fr

April–September, every 45 minutes 10:15am–7pm, every 20 minutes 7–11pm; October–March, every hour 11am–9pm, from 10:15am on weekends

Adults 11€; 11 and under 5,5€; free for under 4

A sightseeing cruise on the river Seine offers a quick overview of Paris's top attractions. Passengers board the Bateaux-Mouches, a company that's been around since 1949, near Port de la Conférence on the right bank, across the river from Invalides, not far from the Champs-Élysées. These one-hour 10-minute rides have recorded (and sometimes difficult to hear) multilingual commentary on sights such as the place de la Concorde, Louvre, Hôtel de Ville, Seine islands, Notre Dame, Musée d'Orsay, and Eiffel Tower. Restrooms are on board and snacks are permitted.

Bois de Boulogne

Entrances at Porte Dauphine, Porte Maillot, Porte d'Auteuil, 16th arr.

08.92.68.30.30

M Porte Dauphine, Porte Maillot, Porte d'Auteuil

www.paris.fr/english

This vast green space on the western edge of the city offers a handful of activities for young ones. It can be a trek depending on where you're staying and is recommended only for those on an extended visit to the city. Inside the park are two man-made lakes, the Lac Supérieur and the Lac Inférieur. At the northern edge of the Lac

Inférieur, families can rent canoes (closest **M** La Muette; 10€/hour plus deposit; March–October 10am–7pm). Stop in for a drink or meal at the charming **Chalet des Îles**, a café-restaurant located on the island in the Lac Inférieur that serves traditional and modern French dishes. Napoléon III gave this Swiss chalet, originally built in Switzerland and transported to France, as a gift to his wife, Eugénie. A small boat also shuttles guests to and from the island every few minutes. The seasonally changing menu can be expensive for dinner, but at lunchtime, there's a two-course (21€) or three-course (27€) set menu. The children's 12€ menu has choices that include squash and chestnut soup, roasted cod, a mini-hamburger, ground poultry burger, green beans, french fries, pasta, and dessert. The English menu can be viewed on the café's website (01.42.88.04.69, www.chalet-des-iles.com).

Jardin de l'Acclimatation

BOIS DE BOULOGNE

inside Bois de Boulogne, 16th arr.
01.40.67.90.85
www.jardindacclimatation.fr
M Les Sablons, Porte Maillot
Daily October–March 10am–6pm; April–September 10am–7pm,
Adults and children 2,9€; free for under 3
Steam-train ride into the amusement park runs every 20 minutes from its station near Porte Maillot Métro station; use Sortie André Maurois (recommended): 2,7€. Individual attractions within the park: 2,7€.

Paris's oldest amusement park, le Jardin de l'Acclimatation in the northern part of the Bois de Boulogne, has been welcoming families since 1860. Children will have fun participating in activities

like visiting farm animals and canoeing on the lake. They'll also love the area with carnival rides—a refreshing reminder that children don't always need state-of-the-art technology to have fun. Animals have been a part of the park since the beginning; the sheep, goats, pigs, donkeys, bulls, and smaller animals live in a farm-like environment here. Kids can get fairly close to and pet the friendlier ones. There's also a huge playground, swings, and a total of eight **cafés** and **snack bars** within the park, including a branch of the famous Angelina tearoom (page 79).

Art, creative movement, and culinary classes in English have been added to the park's repertoire of activities in a partnership with the English-language school, Language Connexion. They are designed for 4- to 12-year-olds and conducted entirely in English. Reservations are required for these Ateliers du Jardin, offered Mondays and Tuesdays 5–6:30pm (to book: 01.40.67.99.05). Information is available in French on the website under the *Les Ateliers Pédagogiques* tab.

Avenue des Champs-Élysées

Place de la Concorde to place Charles de Gaulle, 8th arr.
M Champs-Élysées-Clemenceau, Franklin D. Roosevelt, George V,
Charles de Gaulle-Étoile

Teenagers, more than younger children, may enjoy strolling Paris's
most animated street with its luxury shops, hotels, and cafés. Many
teens find the general bustle of this busy boulevard alluring—it's
easy to slip unnoticed into a noisy, crowded café, sip a *citron pressé*
(fresh-squeezed lemonade) or *Perrier menthe* (Perrier with sweet
mint syrup), and enjoy the unparalleled people-watching vantage.
On the avenue, the relatively inexpensive European clothing chains
Zara and H&M have sizable departments for teens and young
adults. Sephora, Virgin Megastore, and Louis Vuitton all have colossal stores, and there are several mega-movie theaters that often
show films in English with French subtitles (VO, Version Originale,
see page 53).

Musée Jacquemart-André

158, boulevard Haussmann, 8th arr.
01.45.62.11.59
M Saint-Philippe-du-Roule, Miromesnil
www.musee-jacquemart-andre.com
Adults 11€; 7–17 years 9,5€; free for under 7. Family offer: free entry
for the 2nd child between 7 and 17 years old with 2 paying adults and
1 paying child.
Daily 10am–6pm; Mondays and Saturdays until 9pm during
exhibitions
Audio guides in English 5€

Housed in a sumptuous 19th-century mansion, this intimate museum is pleasantly manageable with children. It provides a glimpse into the spectacular home and life of a wealthy art-collecting couple. Kids may respond to the idea of being inside of a home more than to the art, but the permanent collection does include work from van Dyck, Rembrandt, Fragonard, Botticelli, and Donatello among others. A discovery booklet in French with games and puzzles is available for children 7 to 12 years old at the ticket counter or in the museum's boutique.

Café Jacquemart-André is fin-de-siècle luxury at its finest. Located in the mansion's dining room, the splendor is unmistakable — rich red drapes, paneled walls, intricate Belgian tapestries, and an 18th-century ceiling fresco by Tiepolo. For lunch there are quiches, salads (including the Nélie: wild greens, marinated eggplant, sweet peppers, jasmine-scented vinaigrette; the Mantegna: spinach leaves, roasted chicken breast, snap peas, ginger, mangoes, grapefruit, honey vinaigrette; the Vigée Lebrun: mixed salad, salmon with dill, shrimp, lemon, steamed potatoes, creamy dill sauce), and a warm plat du jour. The brunch menu features *viennoiseries*, baked eggs, pastries, salad, smoked salmon, coffee, and juice. The café's terrace is an elegant spot for tea or for enjoying coffee and an afternoon pastry. Reservations are not accepted and the restaurant fills quickly; arrive early or plan to wait in line during peak season. The café's menu is available online in English. Daily 11:45am–5:30pm. Lunch is served from 11:45am–3pm (16,5€ set menu or à la carte); tea service 3–5:30pm (9€); brunch, Saturday, and Sunday 11am–3pm (28€).

Musée Marmottan Monet

2, rue Louis-Boilly, 16th arr.

01.44.96.50.33

M La Muette

www.marmottan.com

Tuesday–Sunday 10am–6pm; Tuesday until 8pm; closed Monday

Adults 10€; 7–25 years 5€; free for under 7

Musée Marmottan Monet houses the largest Monet collection in the world. The museum isn't necessarily of interest to most children, but if it's on a parent's To Do list, children could certainly go along and wouldn't be out of place. The museum's size, within what was formerly a private mansion, makes it easy to see with children. It's located in a quiet area near the edge of the city, about a 10-minute walk from the Métro station through the Jardins du Ranelagh park. Kids who have seen Impressionist art may recognize Monet's late water lily paintings, displayed in the museum's circular room that was built specifically for the canvases.

Parc Monceau

35, boulevard Courcelles, 8th arr.

M Monceau

www.paris.fr

Daily 7am–sunset

This sprawling park, a 10-minute walk north of the Champs-Élysées, is popular with those who prefer a less manicured, more natural look to a public garden. Children and adults picnic, exercise, and play with abandon on the lawns. There are plenty of children's activities including swings, sandboxes, a playground, a duck pond, and a carousel. The Chalet de Monceau kiosk sells snacks, candy, and ice cream.

Le Théâtre du Vrai Guignolet

Rond Point des Champs-Élysées, 8th arr.

01.42.45.38.30

M Champs-Élysées-Clemenceau, Franklin D. Roosevelt

www.theatreguignol.fr

Wednesdays, Saturdays, Sundays, holidays and school vacations at 3pm, 4pm, and 5pm

4€ per person

Tucked into one corner of the park where the avenues Matignon and Gabriel meet is Paris's oldest puppet theater, created in 1818, Le

Théâtre du Vrai Guignolet. Les Marionnettes des Champs-Élysées puppet troupe perform in this charming, outdoor venue. Apart from the theatre, there are old-fashioned swings (1€ for 5 minutes), a playground, a sandbox, and a snack bar in the park. There's also a public **restroom** and **WC** *cabine* nearby, close to the Théâtre Marigny.

Chez Clément

47, avenue de Wagram, 17th arr.

01.53.81.97.00

M Charles de Gaulle-Étoile

www.chezclement.com

Monday–Sunday noon–11:30pm

Chez Clément specializes in traditional French cuisine and is known for its rôtisserie-cooked meats. The décor is cozy-French-farmhouse, which creates an agreeable ambience despite being a chain, especially for visitors. It's one of the best bets in terms of food and service reliability among the sit-down-style chains in France. On the 2-course, 22€ or 3-course, 28€ menu: escargots, foie gras, and terrine de boeuf (starters); roasted pork, roast chicken, steak tartare, poule au pot, and roasted fish (mains); crème brulée or mousse au chocolat (dessert). Kids' menus range from 6€–13€ with mains such as pasta with ham and emmental cheese, beef patty (*steak haché*, Charolais beef), salmon steak, roasted chicken or fish; reservations can be made through the website. There are eight locations in Paris proper.

Additional locations: 123, avenue des Champs-Élysées, 8th arr., **M** George V; 19, boulevard Beaumarchais, 4th arr., **M** Bastille.

Il Caffe Pasta Bar

5, avenue Myron Herrick, 8th arr.

01.42.25.02.70

M Saint-Phillipe-du-Roule

Monday–Friday 8:30am–4pm

Simple, fresh pastas (tagliatelle with red pesto; fettucine with peas and ricotta with herbs), salads (carpaccio with arugula; spinach with fresh goat cheese, peppers, marinated artichokes, pine nuts; lentils, shallots, and coriander), sandwiches (chicken club; tuna and olive tramezzini; ham, mozzarella, olive tapenade, and arugula), and an 11€ lunchtime prix-fixe menu attract many locals. The terrace at this café, located three minutes walking distance from Musée Jacquemart-André, is packed during lunch, but service is relatively fast and tables turn over quickly.

Additional location: 23, rue des Capucines, 1st arr., **M** Opéra, Madeleine.

Jour

12, rue Clément-Marot, 8th arr.

01.49.52.00.75

M Franklin D. Roosevelt, Alma-Marceau

www.jour.fr

Monday–Saturday 11:45am–4:30pm

This popular branch of Jour, a restaurant that serves salads *sur mesur*, is one of 13 locations in Paris proper. Apart from made-to-order salads, wraps, sandwiches, savory tartes, and soups are on the menu (4€–9€, average salad *sur mesur* 10€).

Naked

40, rue du Colisée, 8th arr.
01.43.59.03.24
M Saint-Philippe-du-Roule, Franklin D. Roosevelt
www.nakedfood.fr
Monday–Friday 10am–4pm

Three minutes from the Rond-Point des Champs-Élysées is Naked, a casual, counter-service eatery where customers order and collect their meal at the counter, then find a seat. Its eco-conscious color palette is soothing, with light wood, green awnings and natural decorative accents. On the menu are simple, fresh choices — bagels, Japanese futomaki rolls, sandwiches, salads, smoothies, desserts — as well as warm dishes, including savory tartes, soups, satay, paella, and risottos (4€–10€).

Rutabaga

3, rue du Commandant Rivière, 8th arr.
01.45.63.43.08
M Saint-Philippe-du-Roule, Miromesnil
www.chez-rutabaga.fr
Monday–Saturday 8am–5pm

In between the Rond-Point des Champs-Élysées and the Musée Jacquemart-André is rue du Commandant Rivière, a small street with a number of options for inexpensive, health-conscious counter-service meals offered by cafés that cater to 20-something professionals who lunch in the area. Rutabaga bills itself as *quick cuisine à la française* and has salads, sandwiches both grilled and cold, soups, desserts, and plats du jour such as roasted chicken and vegetarian lasagna (4€–9€).

Additional location: 16, rue des Petits Champs, 2nd arr., **M** Pyramides.

SHOP

Stores on the avenue des Champs-Élysées

On the avenue des Champs-Élysées itself there are a handful of addresses of interest to parents: Point WC, #26, provides customers with clean **restrooms** and a baby changing station; Spanish retailer Zara, at #44, has a children's section upstairs with chic styles at reasonable prices. Also at #44 is the Disney Store, which can offer a useful dose of familiarity for a homesick child who is fond of the brand (**M** Franklin D. Roosevelt). The ubiquitous European H&M department store is at #88 and can come in handy if luggage has been lost and the kids are in need of inexpensive replacement clothes; #114 is the flagship store for IKKS; Petit Bateau is at #116; the enormous Gap store, at #36, has sections for both BabyGap and GapKids.

Stores on avenue Montaigne

Children's fashion is also represented on avenue Montaigne, known for its collection of haute couture design houses. Bonpoint's boutique, nestled in at #49, is well stocked with its latest collections; Baby Dior has a shop within the iconic fashion complex at 26–28, avenue Montaigne.

STAY

Hôtel Élysées Regencia

41, avenue Marceau, 16th arr.

01.47.20.42.65

M George V

www.regencia.com

Elevator/AC/Wifi

Triples from 290€

Five minutes from both the Arc de Triomphe and shopping on the Champs-Élysées, the 4-star Regencia hotel is well-situated within this exclusive district. Rooms and bathrooms are modern and comfortably sized. For families there are several options: triples, suites, and connecting family rooms (from 290€–730€).

Hôtel Keppler

10, rue Kepler, 16th arr.

01.47.20.65.05

M George V

www.keppler.fr

Elevator/AC/Wifi

Suites from 559€

Modern, sophisticated, and comfortable, Hôtel Keppler has four classes of spacious suites, all of which can accommodate two adults and two children under 12 years old, or three adults. The 345-square-foot Traditionelle and Superieure suites are the same size, but the latter has a balcony with views (559€, 609€); the Deluxe suite is a bit larger and enjoys a terrace with an outstanding view of the city and Eiffel Tower (659€). The Penthouse apartment is as luxurious as its name, with two bedrooms and two bathrooms and a spectacular view (809€). Other amenities include a fitness room, sauna, and hammam. Hôtel Keppler provides an alternative to international luxury chains to those looking for a more personalized experience in Paris.

Hôtel Plaza Athénée

25, avenue Montaigne, 8th arr.
01.53.67.66.65
M Franklin D. Roosevelt
www.plaza-athenee-paris.com
Elevator/AC/Wifi
Suites from 1160€

With its long history of attracting a wealthy, fashionable, and titled clientele, the sumptuous Plaza Athénée typifies the ideal of Parisian elegance. Situated between the Champs-Élysées and the Eiffel Tower,

Courtesy Hôtel Plaza Athénée

the location has been synonymous with Haute Couture since it opened in 1911. From the central courtyard's transformation into an ice rink in December and January, to the special menus that use pictures to illustrate children's meals, to the cookies and milk that await little ones upon their arrival, the Plaza has developed a number of creative ways to cater to its younger guests. The hotel has 45 suites that range in size from 500 to 1600 square feet with a Royal suite that measures in at triple that size (from 1160€–10,000€, Royal Suite from 22,000€). The majority of other rooms are connecting, an amenity that opens up many possibilities for families (1385€ to 1535€ for connecting rooms). The history and elegance of this palace hotel make it a splurge-worthy indulgence; it's one of the few grand hotels in Paris that understands the importance of pleasing children as much as their parents.

Hôtel Royal Magda Étoile

7, rue Troyon, 17th arr.
01.47.64.10.19
M Charles de Gaulle-Étoile
www.paris-hotel-magda.com
Elevator/AC/Wifi
Doubles from 200€

This 3-star boutique hotel, accessible from avenue de Wagram off of place Charles de Gaulle, is located on a quiet street that feels far from the bustle of the area, but is really only minutes from the neighborhood's restaurants, cafés, and shopping. Family rooms, configured with a bed and sleeper sofa, accommodate a family of four, as do the larger Junior Suites (200€). Deluxe Suites, with more than 300 square feet of space, offer guests a separate bedroom and living room (220€).

PLAY

EAT

PLAY

Cité des Enfants
Inside the Cité des Sciences et de l'Industrie
30, avenue Corentin-Cariou, 19th arr.
01.40.05.70.00
M Porte de la Villette
www.cite-sciences.fr
Tuesday–Saturday 10am–6pm; Sunday 10am–7pm; closed Tuesday
Cité des Enfants: adults 8€; under 25 6€; free for kids 2 years and younger accompanying another ticketed child

The Cité is a hands-on science and technology center with a planetarium, aquarium, and La Géode, an imposing silver sphere that houses an IMAX theatre (www.lageode.fr). It's a trek from central Paris to this science complex, but the indoor, interactive children's discovery center, the Cité des Enfants, is a fun diversion on a rainy or sweltering day. Children love the chance to don a waterproof smock and play in a series of streams; in a separate area, they can work in a construction zone with play equipment and huge, foam blocks. Two interactive sections are organized, one for kids 2 to 7 years old, the other for 5- to 12-year-olds.

Tickets with entrance times for specific 90-minute sessions, 75 minutes during school vacations, can be purchased online, then printed at kiosks at the center. Meal venues include a sit-down **restaurant**, **pasta bar**, **cafeteria**, and several **snack bars**. Outside, there are French **fast-food venues** like Quick and Hippopotamus as well as ethnic choices.

Cité de la Musique and Musée de la Musique

221, avenue Jean-Jaurès, 19th arr.

01.44.84.44.84

M Porte de Pantin

www.cite-musique.fr

Tuesday–Saturday noon–6pm; Sunday 10am–6pm

Adults 8€; free for under 26

The Cité de la Musique, a music lover's dream, is situated on the opposite side of Parc de la Villette from the Cité des Sciences. It exhibits musical instruments from around the world on five floors, including a collection of five Stradivarius violins. An audio guide, included with admission, allows visitors to hear the sound of each instrument as well as musical selections. Visit-workshops in French, typically held for children 4 to 11 years old on Wednesdays, weekends, and school holidays, introduce kids to both classic and obscure instruments, and give them the opportunity to manipulate them. Because of the hands-on nature of these sessions, they can be appropriate for kids who aren't bilingual. The schedule for workshops, concerts, and other activities is available on the French version of the museum's website under the *Jeune Public* tab.

Parc des Buttes-Chaumont

Entrances on rue Manin, rue Botzaris, rue de Crimée, 19th arr.

M Buttes Chaumont, Laumière, Botzaris

www.paris.fr

Daily 7am–sunset

Parc des Buttes-Chaumont is a magical garden, one often missed by visitors on short stays in the city. It's worth the trip out to Belleville in northeastern Paris however, for a less manicured, less bourgeois experience than what you'll find in the central parks. Rocky buttes, sweeping trees, a mysterious grotto, an artificial waterfall, and the curious Temple de la Sibylle located high atop a peak on a small island in the middle of the lake add to an aura of both fantasy and romance. The temple is accessed by two bridges—older children will certainly appreciate the adventure of crossing the stone bridge 70 feet above the water; a lower-lying suspension bridge provides the second option.

Two well-equipped playgrounds, swings, and a carousel make wonderful playtime choices. Pony rides are available Wednesdays, weekends, and holidays from 3–6pm (2,7€, www.animaponey.com). Le Guignol de Paris, a covered puppet theatre with an entrance at the intersection of avenue Simon Bolivar and rue Botzaris, produces familiar shows like Snow White and the Seven Dwarfs, Aladdin and the Magic Lamp, and Little Red Riding Hood on Wednesdays, weekends, and holidays at 4pm and 5pm (06.98.99.66.24, www.guignolrank.com). Apart from three **restaurants** inside the park, there is space for picnics on the sprawling lawns and **food vendors** sell crêpes, cotton candy, and other goodies around the lake.

Parc de la Villette

Place de la Porte de Pantin, 19th arr.
01.40.03.75.75
M Porte de Pantin, Porte de la Villette
www.villette.com

Located in a northwestern party of the city, the Parc de la Villette is one of Paris's largest parks and recreation areas. It has a number of playgrounds and gardens. In summer, the Bassin de la Villette, between place de la Bataille de Stalingrad and the Pont de Crimée, becomes a center for aquatic activities where families can rent paddleboats, canoes, kayaks, and electric boats. During the popular Paris Plages festival in mid-summer (see page 33), sand is brought in to transform the banks of the Seine into a beach and there's a significant concentration of activities around the Bassin. Outdoor concerts and attractions are a mainstay of the month-long festival (www.paris.fr).

At sunset in July and August, the Cinéma en Plein Air program converts a portion of la Villette into an outdoor movie theatre. Parisians and visitors bring or rent lawn chairs and blankets and watch movies projected on a huge screen. Films are free and shown in Version Originale (www.villette.com). A useful map (*le plan*) can be downloaded from the website under the *Villette Pratique*, then *Accès* tabs.

La Bonne Franquette

2, rue des Saules, 18th arr.

01.42.52.02.42

M Pigalle, Anvers, Blanche, Abbesses, Lamarck-Caulaincourt

www.labonnefranquette.com

Daily 12pm–2pm; 7pm–10pm

La Bonne Franquette is a surprisingly good restaurant, given its touristy location, with a pleasant terrace. Picasso, Renoir, Cézanne, Monet, Toulouse-Lautrec, and many other 19th-century artists frequented this spot. Inspired by its garden, van Gogh painted *La*

Guinguette à Montmartre, which now hangs in Musée d'Orsay. It serves French bistro fare with *tradition du terroir* selections (with suppliers listed on the website) and an *assiette végétarienne*. There's no children's menu, but the traditional menu has several dishes that are sure to please.

Le Coquelicot

24, rue des Abbesses, 18th arr.
01.46.06.18.77
M Abesses
www.coquelicot-montmartre.com
Tuesday–Sunday 7:30am–8pm; breakfast from 8am

Seating is available indoors or outside on the terrace of Le Coquelicot, where breakfast and weekend brunch are offered all day (4–20€). Coquelicot serves coffee, tea, or hot chocolate in bowls, the way one would drink them at home in France. Also on the menu are tartines slathered in homemade jam, artisan yogurt, eggs, bacon, sausage, and fresh juices. Lunch fare is on the light side: fresh salads, fougasses, croques, quiches, omelettes, even a hamburger.

SHOP

Le Ciel est à tout le monde

7, avenue Trudaine, 9th arr.

01.48.78.93.40

M Anvers

cielestatoutlemonde.free.fr

Tuesday–Saturday 10:30am–2pm, 2:45–7pm

Toys

Between the base of Montmartre and the Notre-Dame-de-Lorette neighborhoods is one of three branches of this whimsical Parisian toy boutique; a fourth store is located in the Fontainebleau suburb. The shelves are filled with stuffed animals, dolls, backpacks, games, and crafts. Ride-ons, mobiles, and adorable melamine tableware themed with European characters like Barbapapa, Babar, Maisy Mouse, and Le Petit Prince, are also sold.

Additional locations: Carrousel du Louvre, 99, rue de Rivoli, 1st arr., **M** Louvre-Rivoli, Palais Royal-Musée du Louvre; 10, rue Gay Lussac, 5th arr., RER: Luxembourg.

Käramell

15, rue des Martyrs, 9th arr.
01.53.21.91.77
M Notre-Dame-de-Lorette
www.karamell.fr
Tuesday–Saturday 11am–8pm; Sunday 10:30am–7pm
Candy

Swedish expat Lena Rosen enchants Parisians with more than 180 varieties of irresistibly displayed candy, most imported from Sweden, in her colorful sweets boutique. The shop also delights customers with Scandinavian novelties such as clogs, shoes, Pippi Longstocking dolls, and books.

Ubè Ule

59, rue Condorcet, 9th arr.
01.45.26.93.63
M Anvers, Pigalle
www.ube-ule.com
Tuesday–Saturday 9:30am–7pm
Clothes, Toys, Décor

This boho, kitschy-chic concept store welcomes families with open arms; it's not, unfortunately, as accommodating to strollers. Space is at a premium because of the variety and number of toys, clothes, shoes, and decorative items such as garlands and mobiles carried by the shop. The owners, designers themselves, sell their own line of clothing for children and expectant mothers. It's a 10-minute walk from Sacré Coeur Basilica and worth a detour especially if en route to the rue des Martyrs market street neighborhood.

STAY

Given its location — a 20-minute or more Métro ride from central Paris — Montmartre is not a convenient location for families to stay. The area surrounding the base of the hill, near Métro Pigalle, is well-known as a red-light district. With the prevalence of adult cabarets and shops, some streets can be quite dicey. The neighborhoods mentioned in this guide's tour of Montmartre and the streets surrounding the white-domed Basilique du Sacré Coeur on top of the hill, however, are generally safe.

Le Mur des je t'aime (I love you wall)

Square Jehan Rictus, place des Abbesses, 18th arr.

M Abbesses

www.lesjetaime.com

Moulin de la Galette

83, rue Lepic, 18th arr.

Le Passe-muraille

place Marcel Aymé

Square Suzanne Buisson

7 *bis*, rue Girardon, 18th arr.

Place du Tertre

Sacré Coeur

35, rue du Chevalier-de-la-Barre, 18th arr.

01.53.41.89.00

M Abbesses, Anvers

sacre-coeur-montmartre.com

Square Marcel Bleustein-Blanchet (formerly Parc de la Turlure)

1, rue de la Bonne, 18th arr.

Funiculaire de Montmartre

Lower station:
place Suzanne Valadon
Upper Station:
rue Cardinal Dubois

M Anvers, Abbesses

6am-12:45am

One Métro ticket per person

Le Petit Train de Montmartre

Departs from place Blanche Métro station and place du Tertre

www.promotrain.fr

Daily 10am-6pm, every 30 minutes; in winter every 45 minutes

Full tour: adults 6€, under 12 3,5€; half tour: adults 3,5€, under 12 3€

Montmartre Carousel

Square Louise-Michel

11am-7:30pm

2€ per person

The Walk

One of the most pleasant ways to visit Montmartre is by taking a child-centered walk that leads through some of the district's richly historic residential neighborhoods, where contemporary artists continue to work and create. This peaceful meander is the antithesis of the agoraphobic-inducing experience of many tourists who exit Anvers Métro station and head up rue de Steinkerque towards the base of the Sacré Coeur basilica. Start by taking a less traveled path from Métro Abbesses.

The first stop on the itinerary is easy to miss. After exiting the Métro Abbesses station, turn around and look behind at the Square Jehan Rictus on place des Abbesses. Inside this discreet garden is the *Le mur des je t'aime* (I love you wall). These three words are written 311 times in 250 different languages on a huge, 33-foot by 13-foot tiled mural. Ask your child to try to find I love you in the language of their liking.

Exiting the square, turn right and walk to rue des Abbesses. If by chance it's time to eat, there is a delightful boulangerie-café, **Le Coquelicot**, a few doors down from the corner. (see page 352).

If it's not mealtime, make a right after exiting the square heading towards rue des Abbesses. Just beyond the corner is the easy-to-overlook Passage des Abbesses (if you've passed Le Coquelicot café, you've gone too far). Enter through the arch and climb four steep flights of stairs. For those with a stroller, skip the *passage* and continue to the next street, rue Ravignan, and turn right. Once at the top of either street, continue on rue Ravignan (or turn left on rue des Trois Frères from Passage des Abbesses, then right on Ravignan) up a dozen or so steps through the shaded, postcard-perfect place Émile Goudeau. On the square, at #13, is the Bateau-Lavoir, where Picasso, Braque, Juan Gris, Matisse, and other artists once lived and worked. Some consider this building where Picasso painted *Les Demoiselles d'Avignon* the birthplace of the Cubist art movement. A fire destroyed the original structure in 1970, but it was rebuilt and today houses artists and their studios.

At the intersection just beyond place Émile Goudeau, turn left on rue d'Orchampt and follow it to rue Lepic. Spend a few minutes at this corner and admire one of the two remaining windmills in Montmartre, at 83, rue Lepic. At one time, more than 30 mills punctuated the hillside of Montmartre. Here, the 17th-century Moulin de la Galette, made famous in one of Renoir's most celebrated paintings, *Bal du Moulin de la Galette* (Musée d'Orsay), sits above a restaurant by the same name. The painting portrays an animated, popular outdoor dance garden in 19th-century Montmartre, frequented by Renoir and other artists.

Rue d'Orchampt becomes rue Girardon after rue Lepic. Continue one block on rue Girardon to rue Norvins where, on the right, is place Marcel Aymé and the curious sculpture, *le Passe-muraille*. Kids don't seem to mind pausing to study the man trapped in the wall. This piece was inspired by a character, from one of French writer Aymé's short stories, who developed the power to walk through walls.

Rue Norvins becomes rue Junot at the intersection of Girardon. There's an entrance to Square Suzanne Buisson off of this street, an inconspicuous neighborhood park-playground with a sandbox, spring riders, and a jungle gym, off of rue Junot. The square is a convenient stop at what is approximately the midpoint of this Montmartre walk. Kids can run freely or stop for a snack. A statue of Saint Denis, patron saint of Paris and France, presides over the park. He is holding his head in his hands — according to legend, after he was decapitated on Montmartre, the martyr picked up his head and carried it as he walked for six miles preaching a sermon.

Head back to rue Norvins continuing beyond *le Passe-muraille*. Norvins leads directly into place du Tertre, Montmartre's main square and one of the capital's most heavily touristed areas. Just off of rue Norvins, before reaching place du Tertre, is rue des Saules. **La Bonne Franquette**, at 2, rue des Saules, once a favorite of 19th-century artists like Picasso, Toulouse-Lautrec and Monet, serves French bistro fare (see page 351).

If the plan is to go directly into place du Tertre, take a deep breath. At this point rue Norvins becomes a street of mediocre restaurants and souvenir shops, culminating in something potentially worse in

the main square. At its worst, place du Tertre is a perverse carica-
ture of a community that once nurtured some of Western culture's
most celebrated artists. In high season, tourists pack this small
square rife with portrait artists, some of them pushy, all of them
overpriced. It's the kind of place a seasoned traveler would want to
barrel through. Off-season when it's less crowded, its charm is more
apparent. For some reason, as fate would have it, children, tweens,
even teens, in my experience, seem to love it.

To avoid or to embrace is the question depending on your child's
reaction to this square. When a youngster is keen on place du Tertre,
it can be a refreshing dose of naiveté — the kind that lightens your
heart, even brings you to your knees. Personally, I had walked, bar-
reled rather, through this square a hundred times. When I visited
with my 6-year-old daughter, I opted to go full out at her behest.
Embracing the square in all its glory, we had her portrait painted.
Today, I am grateful that the sweet spirit of that moment was cap-
tured on paper.

Exiting the place du Tertre via rue Norvins, the peak of the white
Byzantine-styled domes of Sacré-Coeur Basilica begin to appear.
Turn left on rue du Mont Cenis, right on souvenir-shop-flanked rue
du Chevalier de la Barre and finally right on rue du Cardinal Guibert
which leads to the Basilica's main plaza. The square is dense with
tourists, hawkers, and scamsters; keep your little ones close. Advise
children to keep their hands at their sides or in their pockets; one
of the most popular scams involves a grinning huckster who blocks
your path and tries to take your hand, quickly weaving a friendship
bracelet on it and demanding payment.

Sacré Coeur Basilica was built as a memorial to French soldiers
who died in the Franco-Prussian war. Although the white church

looks ancient, it was completed only a century ago in 1914. Sacré Coeur (Sacred Heart) is open daily from 6am-10:30pm, with the last entrance at 10:15pm. The view of Paris from this vantage, on one of its highest hills, is breathtaking.

The dome is open to tourists from 9am-7pm, until 6pm in winter. There is a **public lavatory** (paying) down the stairs on rue Lamarck which is on the right side when facing the church; Lamarck is also accessible from rue du Cardinal Dubois, the street in front of the cathedral where the upper funicular station is located.

In the midst of what can be a chaotic area is a tiny, often-forgotten park-playground, Square Marcel Bleustein-Blanchet (formerly Parc de la Turlure), at the corner of rue du Chevalier de la Barre and rue de la Bonne. Leaving place du Tertre on rue Norvins, turn left on rue du Mont Cenis and right on rue du Chevalier de la Barre following it to the left. The street leads to one of the most romantic gardens in the city; children will love its playground with a slide, climbing walls, sand-box, and spring riders, and parents will enjoy the stunning view from this tiered garden. To reach Sacré Coeur from the park, be sure to head back the way you came, following Chevalier de la Barre as it becomes Cardinal Guibert (weekdays 8am–sunset; weekends 9am–sunset).

There are a few options for descending (and ascending) the hundreds of stairs that lead to Sacré Coeur. The stairs themselves, which are always easier heading downhill, are a fun way to descend with children (difficult with toddlers). The Funiculaire de Montmartre is an auto-matic railway that requires one Métro ticket to ride in each direction. It carries more than 6,000 passengers up and down the hill each day between 6am and 12:45am. It doesn't eliminate all of the stairs, but in 90 seconds, visitors can skip 220 of them. The lower station (Gare

Sarah Soetenga

Basse) is located off of place Suzanne Valadon, west of place Saint-Pierre when facing the basilica. Passengers descend at the upper station (Gare Haute) on rue Cardinal Dubois. There are *cabine* toilets nearby.

The touristy, but sometimes more practical way to visit the highlights of Montmartre with young children, is on Le Petit Train de Montmartre. The little white train leaves from the place Blanche Métro station or place du Tertre for a 35-minute bilingual tour that includes drive-bys of sights like the Moulin Rouge, Lapin Agile cabaret, and Montmartre's vineyard among others. Once at the base of the hill in Square Louise-Michel, there is an antique, two-story carousel; it's the one seen in the French film *Amélie*. This vintage merry-go-round is a joyful way to either end, or begin, the trek around memorable Montmartre.

PLAY

Outside of Paris

Château Vaux le Vicomte

Domaine de Vaux le Vicomte, Maincy, 77950

01.64.14.41.90

www.vaux-le-vicomte.com

Open daily, mid-March to mid-December 10am–6pm and during the winter holidays. Saturdays, May–October 8pm–12am, for candlelight evenings. Visit includes the château, garden, and carriage museum. Adults 14€; 6–16 years old and students 11€; free for under 6; family rate 44€, for 2 adults and 2 children.

Audio guides in English: 2€

Vaux le Vicomte is a splendid château, located about 55km southeast of Paris, which provided the inspiration for the Château de Versailles. It was built for Nicolas Fouquet, Louis XIV's superintendent of finances, between 1658 and 1661. Fouquet became a victim of his own good taste after hosting an over-the-top celebration in honor of the King on the grounds of this lavish estate. The extravagant fête fueled suspicion in the monarch and his advisors, who accused Fouquet of a misappropriation of public funds. Fouquet was arrested and imprisoned for life. The King then confiscated what he wanted from the estate and engaged the same team organized by Fouquet—architect Louis Le Vau, decorator Charles Le Brun, and landscape architect André Le Nôtre—to design an even grander palace for himself, Versailles.

Vaux le Vicomte has a number of fun activities for children: period-costume rental lets 2- to 12-year-old boys and girls visit the castle in style (4€); kids are given activity books in English to use as they tour the castle; the lovely, on-site restaurant offers coloring pages and a children's menu; golf carts can be rented to tour the gardens (seats 4, 15€ for 45 minutes). Visitors of any age will be particularly impressed by the sumptuously decorated King's room and Salon des Muses. From May to October, fireworks light up the estate on the first and third Saturday of the month at 10:30pm. In winter, the holidays are celebrated at the château with sparkling lights and festive decorations.

Plan on a full day's trip when heading to Vaux le Vicomte. To reach the château from Paris, take the RER D line from Gare de Lyon (direct train) or Châtelet-Les Halles (longer route) to Melun. From April to November on weekends and holidays, a shuttle bus runs from the station to the château (7€ RT per person). Taxis for up to four people are also available at Melun train station (01.64.52.51.50; 15€ OW during the day; 19€ OW on evenings and Sundays). The château's staff will arrange a return taxi on your behalf.

Château de Versailles

Place d'Armes, 78000 Versailles
01.30.83.78.00
www.chateauversailles.fr
Ticket options: *Le Passeport* gives admission to all Palace tours including the musical fountain shows (*Jardins Musicaux*) and exhibitions; adults 18€, days with shows 25€; free for under 18. *Billet Château* allows access to the castle's most famous rooms and includes exhibitions; adults 15€; free for under 18.
Tickets for the Trianon Palaces and Marie-Antoinette's Estate: adults 10€; free for under 18.
Guided tours in English give access to areas within the château unavailable to the general public such as the Royal Opera and Royal Chapel. Private tours can be especially enjoyable for high school-aged children. Tickets for guided visits for 10- to 25-year-olds can be

purchased only at Versailles; adults 16€; 10–25 years 7€ (7€ also for those who have purchased *Le Passeport* ticket). Audio guides in English for the castle are included in the ticket price; they are available for visitors 8 years and older.

Château open April–October, Tuesday–Sunday 9:30am–6:30pm; November–March, Tuesday–Sunday 9am–5:30pm. Hours for the Queen's Estate, April–October: noon–6:30pm; November–March: noon–5:30pm.

Access to the gardens is free except on musical fountain days: *Les Jardins Musicaux*: Tuesdays from April–October; *Les Grandes Eaux Musicales*: Saturday–Sunday from April–October and Tuesdays May–June; *Les Grandes Eaux Nocturnes*: Saturdays in July–August. Gardens open April–October from 9am–8:30pm; November–March 9am–6pm.

A visit to this magnificent castle and garden estate is as daunting for children as it is for most adults. Families who decide to take their wee ones to the Sun King's residence should arrive early before the doors open, especially in summer months when queue time can reach two to three hours on busy days. With all of those visitors inside, the château can be crowded and uncomfortably hot. Plan on seeing a few selective spaces like the King and Queen's grand apartments, the Hall of Mirrors, and the gardens and fountains immediate to the palace. Strollers are not allowed inside the château, but slings and carriers without a metal frame are permitted for babies. Prepare to wait in more lines at the checkroom, as strollers and any picnic provisions that may have been packed must be left there.

Kids will undoubtedly enjoy visiting Marie Antoinette's rustic hamlet but because of its distance from the château, it's best to visit on a different day. The buildings here are closed to the public but the bucolic fantasy feel to the grounds make the trip worthwhile. It's a great spot to enjoy a picnic; locals like to save their extra bread for the ducks in the pond. What is normally a 25-to-40-minute trip by foot to the Queen's estate is made faster and more accessible with kids by riding the mini-train. Private golf carts and bicycles are also available to rent. For those who have a full day slated for Versailles and want to attempt to see everything, children, especially the youngest ones, will be forever grateful to parents who take advantage of one of the transportation services. Trains leave from the Terrasse Nord (www.train-versailles.com, adults 6,70€; 11–18 years 5,20€; under 11 free). One exception, on days when the Grandes Eaux spectacle takes place, only visitors with a palace *Passeport* or a Grandes Eaux Musicales ticket can purchase mini-train ride tickets. If a family has only a week in Paris, a trip to Versailles might not be the best use of time: it takes a day to see, and a day to recover.

From Paris take the RER C line to Versailles-Rive Gauche (zones 1–4). For the most expedient trip, board a train whose name begins with "V." As always, the RER ticket is required to exit the station, so keep it handy—small tickets are easy to lose when your hands are full. It's a 5-minute walk from the station to the Versailles estate. **Restrooms** with diaper-changing facilities are located near the entrance to the château and the gardens. An interactive map detailing picnic spots, restrooms, restaurants, and activities is available on the website. Versailles has many choices for food on its grounds: **snack stands**, **cafés**, and **restaurants** that include the famous and luxe Parisian **tea salons**, Angelina and Ladurée. In summer, boats can be rented for use in the Grand Canal and there are pony rides nearby (see the online map for detailed locations).

Disneyland Paris and Walt Disney Studios Theme Parks

Marne-la-Vallée, 77705
01.60.30.60.53
RER A4 to Marne-la-Vallée/Chessy station
us.disneylandparis.com
Parks open daily at 10am, closing times vary between 6pm to 9pm, depending on the day of week. Adults 1-day ticket 81€; 3–11 years 73€; 2 and under free. Multiple-day passes are available; significant discounts are offered on advance-purchase tickets bought online.

It's a simple, straightforward 35-minute trek on RER A4 to Disneyland Paris's front gate. The two parks, Disneyland and Walt Disney Studios, are accessible with the same ticket. Disneyland is divided into five areas: Adventureland, Discoveryland, Fantasyland, Frontierland, and Main Street U.S.A. The parks have convenient amenities for families with young children: stroller rental, changing tables, high chairs in restaurants, and equipment to warm bottles and baby food. Ask about Baby Switch, a perk that lets parents whose children are too young to ride with them on an attraction, take turns without waiting in line twice. Highlights among the two parks' 56 attractions include Toon Studio, the Pirates of the Caribbean ride, the Rock 'n' Roller Coaster, and Space Mountain: Mission 2. Disney Village, situated between the parks and Disney hotels, is an entertainment district with restaurants, dancing, shopping, and a huge movie and IMAX theater complex.

Musée de l'Air et de l'Éspace

Aéroport de Paris, Le Bourget BP 173, Le Bourget 93352
01.49.92.70.62
www.mae.org

M La Corneuve, then bus #152 to Musée de l'Air et de l'Éspace. Accessible by bus #350 from Gare de l'Est, Gare du Nord, Place de la Chapelle, or Porte de la Chapelle Métro stations.

April–September, Tuesday–Sunday 10am–6pm; October–March, 10am–5pm. Visits to the permanent collection are free of charge. France's air and space museum is a fascinating, off-path find for fans of aviation. Le Bourget is Paris's former main airport and the spot where Charles Lindbergh landed the Spirit of St. Louis in 1927, after completing the world's first solo, nonstop, transatlantic flight. Exhibits trace the development of air travel from balloons and the first flying machines to airplanes from WWI and WWII to rockets and spacecraft. On the tarmac, two Concorde planes are open to tour as is a Boeing 747. **L'Hélice** is the on-site restaurant and a good option for refueling; families can also pack a picnic to eat on the grounds.

Musée Vivant du Cheval

Grandes Écuries, Château de Chantilly
Chantilly, 60500
03.44.27.31.80
www.museevivantducheval.fr; www.chateaudechantilly.com
April–October, Monday and Wednesday–Sunday 10am–5pm;
January–March, Monday and Wednesday–Sunday 1:30–5pm
Adults 11€; 4–17 years 4,5€; 3 and under free
From Paris's Châtelet-Les Halles station, take the RER line D to the

Chantilly-Gouvieux stop (45 minutes). From the train station, it's a 5-minute ride to the château (8€). The free local shuttle, le DUC, also transports tourists from the station—get off at the Chantilly-Église Notre Dame stop. The shuttle schedule is available on the museum's website.

The horses are the real attraction of this living museum. Children have a chance to get up close and personal with the 30 pampered ponies that belong to the museum. Forty-five-minute dressage demonstrations are held each day from January to October at 11am and/or 2:30pm except on show days. A one-hour holiday equestrian show is organized on weekends at 2:30pm and/or 4:30pm during the month of December (adults 29,5€; 4–17 years 16,5€). In high season an elaborate horse show is hosted Thursdays through Sundays at 2:30pm. The schedule changes by season; check the website for exact opening times and show times. Although its exact origin is disputed, legend has it that whipped cream (crème de Chantilly) was invented here in the 17th century; two **restaurants** on the château grounds offer the chance to sample it.

Parc Astérix

Plailly, BP 8 60128
03.44.62.34.34
www.parcasterix.fr

Astérix shuttle buses leave every 30 minutes from 9am to 7pm, from Charles de Gaulle Terminals 1 and 3 (5,20€–6,90€). In high season, shuttles depart from the Louvre and the Eiffel Tower at 8:45am and return at 6:30pm (20€). Open daily from early April–October 10am–6pm; closing times vary depending on the day; see website for exact hours.

Adults 40€; 3–12 years 30€; 2 and under free

Parc Astérix is Paris's other large amusement park, named after one of France's most beloved comic book characters, Astérix the Gaul. The stories follow the comic adventures of Astérix and Obélix, two brave warriors who successfully resist Roman occupation. The park is seasonal, open primarily in summer and during weekends and school vacations in the fall. It may not be the well-oiled machine of Disney, but with its uniquely French theme, it has its charm. Inside are five lands: Gaul, the Roman Empire, Greece, Vikings, and Travel Through Time, a mishmash of different eras. The park has 31 rides, including the Tonnerre de Zeus, an enormous wooden roller coaster that reaches speeds of 50 mph. Six shows entertain visitors; one of the most popular is the outdoor water show featuring live dolphins.

RESTROOMS OPEN TO THE PUBLIC

PLAYGROUNDS

CAROUSELS

ABOUT THE AUTHOR

Kim Horton Levesque is a travel writer and French translator with a background in teaching and journalism. She spent many years studying, traveling, and working in France and Western Europe and continues to be an avid traveler. She lives in Phoenix, Arizona, with her family.